Ronald Seth (1911–1985) was educated in Ely and Cambridge. After his studies at Cambridge he went to Tallin University, Estonia, where he held the English Language chair and received an honorary Ph.D in 1939. When war broke out, he helped found the Intelligence Bureau of the B.B.C. Monitoring Service and was then seconded to Special Operations Executive. He was assigned the task of working covertly in Estonia to organise resistance against the Nazis. Betrayed and captured, he endured solitary confinement for almost two years but, during that time, persuaded his captors he was a Nazi sympathiser. He joined Luftwaffe Intelligence, where he was exposed constantly to the danger of losing the trust of Nazi officials. Smuggled into Paris in 1944, he was taken back to Germany, from where he was able to return to Britain under the pretext of a mission. After the war, he was employed by the Ministry of Works, became a school teacher for a time, and eventually devoted himself to a writing career.

'Ein Spion hat keinen Kameraden'

From a German manual for secret agents

RONALD SETH

A SPY HAS NO FRIENDS

TO SAVE HIS COUNTRY, HE BECAME THE ENEMY

headline
review

First published in 1952 by Andre Deutsch

This edition published in 2008
by HEADLINE REVIEW

An imprint of HEADLINE PUBLISHING GROUP

1

Cataloguing in Publication Data is available from the British Library

ISBN 978 07553 1805 6

Typeset in Perpetua by Palimpsest Book Production Ltd, Grangemouth, Stirlingshire

Printed and bound in Great Britain by Mackays of Chatham plc, Chatham, Kent

Headline's policy is to use papers that are natural, renewable and recyclable
products and made from wood grown in sustainable forests. The
logging and manufacturing processes are expected to conform to
the environmental regulations of the country of origin.

HEADLINE PUBLISHING GROUP
An Hachette Livre UK Company
338 Euston Road
London NW1 3BH

www.headline.co.uk
www.hachettelivre.co.uk

CONTENTS

Headline would like to thank the family of Ronald Seth for their assistance in preparing the material included in the appendix, and for providing 'Levavi Oculos'.

AUTHOR'S NOTE

The fortunes of war throw many people into associations which they would otherwise be careful to avoid. Some of those who befriended me in Paris at great risk to themselves, and to whom I owe an everlasting debt of gratitude, were forced by circumstances into close association with a group of collaborators. Members of this group certainly incurred the suspicions of their neighbours, though some of them may have escaped their deserts. In order to spare the feelings of people innocently associated with them, I have given fictitious names and addresses to everyone with whom this part of my story deals. Apart from these few changes, I have kept as strictly to the truth as my memory would allow, aided by such notes as I was able to preserve.

1952

CHAPTER I

OPERATION BLUNDERHEAD
BEGINS

I WAS awakened suddenly by a jerk; with the return of consciousness my ears were filled with the droning of the aircraft. I opened my eyes to find the parachute despatcher standing over me. He was shaking me by the shoulder and holding out a mug of coffee.

'We are just passing over Bornholm,' he shouted. 'We shall be over the target in an hour. Drink this, and eat these sandwiches; and here are two bars of chocolate and a packet of gums to put in your pocket.'

I was feeling slightly sick and did not want either the coffee or the sandwiches. I was not really awake, and felt numbed all over. Then suddenly the meaning of the despatcher's words cleared my mind, and there came over me a feeling of great fear. In less than an hour I might be dead; and I did not want to die. There was much in my life that I still longed to do, much that I wanted to undo. I began to pray and to make to the Almighty promises which I knew I could never fulfil.

In what seemed like a few minutes, though it must have been almost an hour later, the despatcher returned to tell me that the Captain would like me to go forward to his cabin. I went forward, and on looking out found that we were over Kolga Bay, a small curving inlet on the north coast of Estonia, fifty miles south of the southern Finnish coast, and less than two hundred miles from Leningrad.

'We will circle once or twice, then I want you to choose where you would like to be put down,' the Captain said.

Below us in the brilliant moonlight I could see the whole Kolga Peninsula spread out, the coast roads looking like white ribbons. In the wrinkled sea I could pick out the huge rock which lay about two hundred yards from the shore opposite my friend Juhan's cottage. A thrill like that of a home-coming went through me as I looked down on this familiar country, where my wife and children and I had been so happy and had made so many friends in the summer before the war.

Away to the east I saw a cloud bank with a base at about fifteen hundred feet. I pointed it out hopefully to the Captain, but he had already seen it. We circled again, and I picked out a field about a mile south of Juhan's cottage. It was skirted on the west by the coast road and on the east by dense forest. I asked the Captain if he could guarantee to put me down, with my three containers of explosives and equipment and the heavy package containing my wireless transmitter, neither in the sea nor in the forest. He said that he most certainly could.

We shook hands, but I asked him not to wish me luck, so he contented himself with giving me final instructions.

'We shall circle once after you have dropped, and immediately you have landed, if everything is O.K., I want you to give three long flashes on your torch. If I don't get them I shall be very sad.'

I clambered back over the main spar and found that the despatcher and the rear-gunner had already opened the hatch in the floor amidships. The despatcher fixed my static-line to the canvas and showed me the pin. The routine we had gone through when I was learning to jump at Tatton Park served to keep me calm. Now that I had something to do, my fear receded. I was trembling a little, but I had always done that before jumping. I sat down on the edge of the hole with my legs dangling in space.

'Keep your eye on the light!' the despatcher shouted. 'As soon as it goes red I shall say: "Action stations! Get ready! Container – container – container – go!" Then the package will follow. God go with you.'

He had hardly finished speaking when the red light flashed. I had no time for wishing to turn back now.

'Container – container – container – go!' yelled the despatcher.

And I went.

I must have caught my parachute pack on the edge of the hole as I went through, because when I came out of that amnesiac second of falling through the slip-stream, I found I was spinning round like a top. What with this motion and my concentration on the lines becoming untwisted, so that I could pull them apart and stop them twisting the opposite way, I had absolutely no idea where my containers had fallen.

The aircraft had gone off to the south, and I could hear its engines faintly throbbing in the distance. But apart from this and far-off sounds of a dog barking and men shouting, there was a deep silence such as I had not heard for a long time. I floated gently downwards.

The barking dog and the shouting men would have thrown me into a cold sweat, only I was so intent on making a good landing that the significance of these sounds did not strike me. I came out of my spin a few seconds before landing, and looked down for the first time. Then I saw that I was heading straight for some telephone wires running by the side of a road; and there waiting for me to land, were a dog and a group of men waving rifles.

Even then I tried to take evasive action in the best R.A.F. Ringway style, but I was unlucky. The lines of my parachute caught the branches of a tree overhanging the wires and I was brought up with a jerk. Gently, softly and with a faint rustle the silken canopy fluttered about me as I swayed to and fro some six feet from the ground, surrounded by four or five soldiers and a very excited dog.

One of the men shouted an order, and then came the answer: '*Jawohl, Herr Feldwebel!*'

I was face to face with the enemy.

Six hours ago I had been dining in a Royal Air Force mess, safe on English soil. Now I was more than twelve hundred miles away, caught in the act of landing by parachute from an aircraft, dressed as a civilian, and with enough explosives in my equipment to blow up a small town — and I was surrounded by armed German soldiers.

I glanced up quickly as I heard the aircraft droning overhead towards the west, but I could not flash my torch. The dog, hysterical with excitement, was leaping from one soldier to another.

I opened my knife to cut myself free, then I remembered the quick release attachment. I turned it and was about to bang the button, keeping my eye on the soldiers, who appeared much more interested in the dog than in me, when suddenly the *Feldwebel* lashed out at the animal with his foot. With a snarl the dog fastened its teeth in the man's leg. Instantly there was confusion. In trying to pull the dog off, one man received a blow on the arm from another who swung his rifle at the beast. In a second I released myself from my harness and began running across the field as fast as my encumbered body could go. The edge of the forest was less than a hundred and fifty yards away. I was about half-way there when suddenly the moon was blotted out, and a moment later rain began to fall as though a cloud had burst.

CHAPTER 2

RETROSPECT

I

IN 1935 I had accepted the appointment of lecturer in English Language and Literature at the University of Tallinn, being subsequently raised to the Chair. In addition to this post I held various others, among them that of Senior Master at the Tõrvand-Tellmann English College, a large co-educational school of eight hundred pupils; English Teacher to the Ministry of Economic Affairs; broadcaster of weekly English lessons over the National Radio; English Language Adviser to the Estonian Foreign Office; and associate editor of the *Baltic Times*. During term-time I worked sixteen hours a day, but I was young and active and the long summer vacations from May to early October provided ample opportunity for recuperation, particularly as the Estonian summer insured ten to twelve weeks of almost unbroken sunshine.

In the summer of 1939 we were living in the Veizenberg'i tänav, near the Kadriorg Park. But our family was growing, and a move was becoming necessary. At the end of term we found a flat in a new block that was still being built; it was due to be available in the following

September. A friend having offered us the use of his seaside cottage for the summer, we stored our furniture in the English College, which was quite near both to the old and the new flats, and went to stay there. After their early timidity had worn off, the local people accepted us, and we became part of the community life.

The cottage stood a hundred yards from the edge of the sea in the tiny fishing village of Kiiu Aabla, on the west side of a small peninsula on the north coast. The peninsula was about six miles long from its northern apex to its base and three miles at its widest. A road followed the west coast to the village of Leetse, about half a mile from the tip, then struck south-east through the forest until it reached the coast, which it then followed south until it joined the main Tallinn road not far from where the west coast road left it. The centre of the peninsula was thick forest, but along the coast roads there were hamlets built on a margin of unforested land about half a mile deep, which could be worked as small holdings. On the produce of these small holdings and the results of their fishing the peasant-fishermen sustained life. Only for meat, sugar and salt and one or two other simple commodities did they have to rely on the town.

My friend Juhan, who had organised to perfection a life in which the least activity was the criterion, lived in one room of the cottage. His sole duty was to milk the cow twice a day, and this done, the rest of the time he spent eating, sleeping and playing his piano accordion.

University entrance examinations necessitated my return to Tallinn on 23rd August 1939. Our new flat was not yet ready, but Madame Tõrvand-Tellmann put her own at our disposal, as she was still at her country house near Kotka. Here we arrived on 22nd August.

Next day came the news of the Russo-German pact. In an hour the threat to Estonia, which the international situation already offered, had changed direction; it now came from the west instead of the east. When I heard the announcement of the German march against Poland, I was convinced that this was the beginning of the general conflagration we had all feared for the last year, and I made up my mind to get my family to England as quickly as possible. This meant my seeking special permission from the Rector and Senate of the University to resign immediately and my asking to be released from my arrangements with Madame Tõrvand-Tellmann, the Foreign Office and the National Radio.

Professor Kogerman, the Rector, expressed keen sympathy with my position, and in less than an hour was able to send me on my way with his own and the Senate's blessing. Hanno Kompas, Director of the Radio, was glum. He was sure this was the end of Estonia. Karl Selter, the Foreign Minister, though much overworked, made time to see me for a quarter of an hour, and thanked me for my assistance. Colonel Jaakson, Minister of Education, also received me, and expressed the Ministry's and his own warm appreciation of my services to education. Only Madame Tõrvand-Tellmann pressed me to stay.

'England and France won't declare war,' she said. 'It will all be over in six weeks.' But when I explained my reasons for leaving she reluctantly let me go.

The earliest date by which we could complete our arrangements would be Tuesday, 5th September. It took us all our time to get ready, for on Monday we had to attend various farewell functions and presentations, at all of which I had to make short speeches. The farewell from the English College was most touching and I concluded my speech with a promise that whatever happened, I would come back. I made this promise seriously and with the firm intention of keeping it. How it was to be kept I had then not the glimmering of an idea.

At half-past nine on Tuesday we boarded the Tallinn-Helsinki steamer — I had bought tickets to Newcastle via Helsinki, Turku, Stockholm, Oslo and Bergen — and promptly at ten o'clock, as the boat pulled away, the eight hundred boys and girls of the English College, who were massed on the quay, sang a wonderful Estonian farewell. When the song was over, shouts of 'Come back to us!' were carried across the water. I tried to repeat my promise of the previous day, but I was so moved that I could only mutter to myself.

We had taken the Estonians and their country to our hearts in a very short time. In no other place in the world had we been so kindly treated. From the moment we arrived people went out of their way to help us and make us feel at home. But we had not realised that we had been so greatly loved and were quite overcome by the affection with which they sent us on our journey.

II

For several weeks I walked the streets of London job-hunting, and eventually joined the B.B.C. as a sub-editor of its daily digest of Foreign Broadcasts. Two months later I helped to found the Intelligence Information Bureau of the Monitoring Service, which later in the war achieved considerable fame.

I stayed with the B.B.C. for a year, during which time I rose to be Chief Intelligence Supervisor (Country); but the constant jockeying for advancement and intrigues, which would make pale the machinations of Queen Anne's court in comparison, proved too much for me, and I resigned. A few weeks later I volunteered for the Royal Air Force, passed through the ranks at Bridgnorth, and in June 1941, became an Intelligence Officer in Bomber Command.

I happened one day to be in the Air Ministry when someone said to me: 'By the way, Seth, you know those shale-oil mines in north-eastern Estonia, which the Russians were supposed to have "scorched"? Well, Jerry has got them going again, and they're producing three hundred tons a day – practically all he needs to support his armour on the Leningrad front.'

For several weeks this thought must have churned about in my subconscious mind, because one morning when I woke up I had a plan worked out for an operation which, if successful, would put the Estonian mines out of commission for some considerable time. Without thinking much more about it I forwarded the scheme to Intelligence, and to my surprise it was accepted. In January 1942, I was seconded from the R.A.F. to Special Operations Executive, better known as S.O.E. Internally, that is to say among the staff and students, it was politely referred to as the 'Organisation', less politely (until an order came round forbidding the term), as the 'Racket'.

The Organisation had a finger in pies of practically every European make, and eventually developed until it covered the Far East as well, in co-operation with the Americans, who learnt most of the craft from us.

Before I finally signed the Official Secrets Act and other documents essential to joining S.O.E., a major, whom I will call Larch, had pointed out that even if my plan were successful, my chances of survival were estimated by the experts at not more than fifteen per cent. Now, therefore, was the time to withdraw, if I felt like doing so. Carried along by conceit, self-confidence and a tinge of patriotism, I rejected the offer with some disdain. I signed the documents without a thought, and Major Larch became my guide, philosopher and friend. My wife, who had placed the children in a nursery school in Devon, joined the W.A.A.F., since I should henceforward be under the closest security régime and so would be able to see very little of her.

As I should be the first British agent in Estonia, and since having got there I should not be able to return until the end of the war, I should have ample opportunity for organising an underground movement for carrying out both passive and active resistance, concentrating on the one railway line from Tallinn to Leningrad. I should also have plenty of leisure for gathering military intelligence.

My training was exhaustive, and involved nearly ten months of extremely hard work. By the middle of September I had passed my final test, and after a short leave with my wife, I went to London with Major Larch to perfect the details of the operation.

First, there was my equipment. This was to consist of an 'A' container, a six-foot-long steel cylinder, full of explosives, detonators and fuses; a second 'A' container loaded with food, in case I could not find Juhan and should have to fend for myself in the forests for a month or six weeks; and a third container holding an Arctic tent, a sleeping bag, three hundred gold marks (long obsolete, but which we hoped would be useful with the peasants), fourteen pounds of chocolate, fourteen pounds of sugar, a number of Colt .32s, with an adequate supply of ammunition, and various odds and ends.

The radio equipment was packed in a separate parcel, about four feet by three by two. This was to follow me through the hole, while the containers would be slung in the bomb-racks and released immediately before me.

My personal kit received the most careful attention. Here I feel I must pay a tribute to Major Larch, who was himself responsible for this most important part of my equipment. The rest was in the hands of officers whose job it was to look after such things. I soon had cause, however, to wish that Larch had superintended the rest of my paraphernalia.

For the jump itself I was to wear a camouflaged canvas siren suit, in the pockets of which were my L tablet — potassium cyanide, guaranteeing death in three minutes, in case anything should go wrong — a packet of clear gums, two two-ounce bars of milk chocolate, and some benzedrine. There was also a torch, and a knife for cutting myself free if anything went wrong with the parachute. A spade was strapped to my left leg. With this I was to bury my parachute and the containers until I had had a look round.

It had been decided that I should go in the October moon-period, otherwise it would be too late; the hard winter weather of Estonia would come down in November and preclude any further attempt until the following spring. As something like £4,000 had been spent on my training up to date, six or eight months delay would add to this expense. I certainly had no desire to wait so long, keyed up and with nothing to do.

I was given a final seven days' leave and my wife joined me in London. She would have had to have been very dull not to have sensed that something more than security work had been occupying my time during all these months. The seven days passed all too quickly, and on Friday, October 16th 1942, I reported to Larch for the last time. It was the first night of the October operational moon-period. If climatic conditions over the target were favourable, tomorrow night I might be in Estonia. If conditions were unfavourable for the whole of the period, I might not go at all.

Larch took me to say goodbye to Brigadier (now Major-General Sir Colin) Gubbins, who was then chief of S.O.E. He shook hands and said, 'Take care of yourself. You are my ewe-lamb in the Baltic. Come and tell me all about it when you get back.'

Later, in Larch's office, before we left London that evening, I was introduced to a young captain of the Lovat Scouts, who henceforth was to be my constant companion until I left, never letting me out of his sight for a moment. Even at the waiting base we slept in the same room.

Nothing happened the next night; nor the next, nor the next. Every day at ten o'clock we received the meteorological report for the day. Sometimes we would be told: 'No operation today.' If there was any doubt there was to be definite news at noon.

At ten o'clock on Saturday, 24th October, we were told: 'Operation Blunderhead is on. Blunderhead is to be ready to take off at any time from noon onwards.' When I had first been told my operational name I had objected a little, with my tongue in my cheek. I had been assured, however, that several names had been put into a hat and drawn.

At eleven o'clock I received from Larch a telegram from my wife telling me that she had been granted her commission. I felt this to be a good omen and was relieved, for I knew that now she would be comparatively happy.

Shortly before noon I drove with my escort to the airfield, where I was introduced to the Polish crew of the Halifax in which I was to fly. As the distance was so great – a round trip of thirteen or fourteen hours, flying partly over enemy-occupied territory – it had been arranged that we should go to an airfield near York for refuelling and final checks.

At five o'clock, after an operational tea of bacon, chips, fried eggs, hot buttered toast and strawberry jam, we drove out to the aircraft. I changed into my operational kit and by five-thirty we were airborne.

Now, seven hours later, I was on the ground in enemy-occupied country, being chased by German soldiers. It was a beginning which we had never dared to consider. The worst had happened, and as I raced for the shelter of the forest I was making that desperate bid which we had hoped I should never have to make.

CHAPTER 3

TWELVE DAYS OF FREEDOM

PURSUIT seemed to give me strength and sight, for in the forest the night was even darker and the undergrowth made it difficult to get along, but I managed to keep going. Shouts behind me were drawing nearer and I could hear the crashing of feet. I paused, crouching under a tree, to get my breath, and turning for a moment towards the sounds, I caught sight of flashing torches. I had little fear that I should be caught now, but I felt it would be safer to find a hideout.

Going a little deeper into the forest I found a tree whose lower branches swept the ground. I hoisted myself up into it and climbed until I was twenty or thirty feet up. Here I found a comfortable fork which seemed a good place to spend the night, and for safety I fastened myself to the trunk.

Presently the noises of my pursuers ceased, and I imagined that the search had been called off. As soon as I realised this a reaction set in and I became intolerably weary, so to ward off sleep I took two benzedrine tablets. I decided that when dawn broke I would go down and try to find my equipment, particularly the radio. I hoped the containers might be lying near some temporary cover, for I could scarcely move them and I did not see how I could possibly bury them in broad daylight without being seen.

The benzedrine was not effective; I became more and more drowsy until at last I fell asleep. When I woke it had stopped raining and there was a faint glimmer of light in the tree-tops. I was stiff and cold and shivering, so I took a gulp of whisky from my flask, which held three-quarters of a pint. I had to strip off the top part of my siren suit to get at it, but it was worth the effort, for the warmth went down into my stomach and diffused itself all over my body.

Picking my way carefully and silently through the under-growth — for I did not know whether guards had been left — I came to the field. There was no one about. On the far side the canopy of my parachute billowed and flapped in the gentle morning breeze coming off the sea.

A shallow ditch went down to the gate and I crawled into it, taking advantage of what little cover the low hedge afforded. When I had gone about half-way I heard voices, and spying through a tuft of grass I watched two German soldiers, who had arrived on bicycles, disentangle my parachute from the tree, roll it up and ride back in the direction from which they had come.

Any reconnoitring I might now do would have to be

done with care. If the local post was stirring, there was no telling who might be about. Taking cover behind a bush I surveyed the field, but could see nothing which resembled a container; nor did the adjoining field reveal anything. I climbed through the hedge and lay in the ditch by the roadside. Daylight was rapidly approaching.

Suddenly I heard the sound of a lorry. It was too late to get back through the hedge, so I scurried along to a bush, hoping it would protect me from the eyes of the driver as he passed me. Then I heard the quicker beat of a motorcycle engine, and a second or two later it came round the bend and pulled up sharply. The rider turned and signalled to the lorry to stop. Then I saw them – two of my containers, in a well-dropped 'stick', straddling the road. I watched them being loaded on to the lorry, which then turned round and drove off.

The whole aspect of my operation was now changed. I was completely without supplies of food or any means of communicating with my base. The only bright spots in my future were the Colt under my arm, the fighting knife in my pocket, and £1,500, in American dollars and Swedish krona, strapped across my chest. What I should do needed thinking over, so I went back to the forest.

Sitting down under a tree on a carpet of pine needles, I ate a couple of clear gums and a square of milk chocolate, which I washed down with a mouthful of whisky.

My plan, as it unfolded, rested on whether I could find Juhan, who would be able to give me a picture of conditions in the country. If these appeared too formidable, I would try to buy or steal a small sailing boat and attempt the three hundred miles to Sweden. From there I could return to England and try again.

It was about eight o'clock when I heard once more the sound of engines. Going to the edge of the forest, I saw three lorries draw up and a party of soldiers with rifles jump out. Presently some officers arrived in a motor car, orders were given and the soldiers deployed.

I retreated into the forest, and having found another suitable tree, I repeated my performance of the previous night. The soldiers beat backwards and forwards through the forest, passing several times below my tree. Now and again a Fieseler-Storch aircraft (the German equivalent of the British Lysander observation aircraft) flew over. All day long I heard the calls and crashings of my searchers. It was a fantastic operation. I do not know whether a similar party was operating from the northern end of the peninsula, but it would have been possible even for a cretin to have eluded capture. This was the first revelation of German military incompetence that I experienced, but it was not to be the last.

Towards five o'clock, as daylight began to fade, whistles blew and the weary soldiery withdrew to their lorries, climbed in and drove off. When the sound of the engines had died away, I climbed down from my tree and restored the circulation to my cramped limbs. There was an uncomfortable emptiness in the pit of my stomach, reminding me that I had not eaten for twenty-four hours. I must find food, I decided, and there was nowhere, unless at a peasant cottage, where I should be likely to do so. I assumed that the inhabitants of the peninsula must know what all the day's activity had been about, and I was confident that I could rely on their hatred of the German invaders inducing them to help me. So I set off in search of a cottage.

I made my way to the road, and with eyes and ears alert for the slightest sound or sight of a uniform, I went towards the north. Two or three hundred yards up the road I came to a cottage and knocked at the door. A very old man opened it and peered out.

'Can you give me something to eat?' I asked him in Estonian. 'Perhaps a little bread or some potatoes and milk?'

He paused before replying, looking at me closely. 'I have nothing,' he said at last, 'but my daughter over there may have something.' He nodded in the direction of another cottage a hundred yards away, then closed the door abruptly and bolted it.

Cautiously I went over to the daughter's cottage. As I came up to the door I could hear women and children talking excitedly, though I could not distinguish what was being said. As soon as I knocked there was silence. After a pause I heard someone moving stealthily on the other side of the door.

'Who's there?' called a woman's voice.

'Please can you give me some bread?' I asked. 'I've eaten nothing since yesterday.'

'Who is it?' I heard another voice whisper.

'*Vōramees,*' answered the first. (The word may mean either a stranger or a foreigner.)

At once the women and children set up a screeching which I was sure would rouse the whole countryside.

'Go away!' called the first woman. I did not wait.

I had walked on a little further, when I saw a woman with two young boys and a girl running across the fields to another house on the other side of the road. They ran indoors, calling out as they went, and as I drew near the house a party of men with rifles ran out.

I leapt into the forest, which at this point came down to the road's edge, and fell flat in the undergrowth, just as a bullet went whining past me. I was sure they had seen me entering the forest, but to my surprise the party ran off down the road in the direction from which I had come, letting off their guns spasmodically as they went.

Shaken by this experience, I went a little deeper into the forest. I had been told that the population would be friendly; but if this was an amiable welcome, I decided that I would not like to meet an unfriendly Estonian. This attitude was certainly going to add to my difficulties. Again I climbed a tree, deciding that in the morning I would make for Juhan's cottage, reconnoitre it and find out if he was still living there. If I could only discover him, I knew he would be my friend. In any case, I must find him in order to get food, for I did not dare to risk approaching strangers again. So I took another mouthful of whisky and then slept.

I woke soon after dawn, and was about to come down from my tree when I heard noises in the undergrowth below. Peering down, I saw two men, one with a spade and the other with a sack on his back. I watched them dig a shallow hole, bury the sack and then go away. When I judged that it was safe for me to do so, I came down, scraped away at the earth and uncovered the sack. In it, to my astonishment, I found eighteen specially prepared charges which had been included in my odds-and-ends container. How they could possibly have got there I could not imagine, and it was not until two years after the end of the war that I discovered a possible explanation.

When I was demobilised I got an appointment in the Ministry of Works Southern Regional Headquarters. Shortly afterwards my chief resigned and I succeeded to the post. My duties here brought me into contact with some of the displaced persons working in the Bedford brickfields, among whom were two or three Estonians, former pupils of mine at the English College in Tallinn. In the early days of May 1948, I received from one of them the following cutting from the Estonian supplement to the *Stockholms Tidningen* of a few days earlier.

AN ENGLISH PARACHUTIST IN OCCUPIED ESTONIA

Many strange things happen in wartime, of which the results sometimes come to light only after hostilities have ended. Such an event, which occurred during the German occupation of Estonia, has been told us by a compatriot, who lived during the war in the commune of Konnu near Loksa.

One dark night in the late autumn of 1942 a local farmer was awakened by a sudden shock which shook the building. Running out of the house, the farm hands found a large cloth dangling from a wall. This they discovered to be a parachute attached to a large box. The box was opened and in it were found tinned food, weapons, aummunition and other articles. It was assumed that they were provisions dropped for a parachutist who was thought to be hiding in the neighbourhood.

The local authorities were informed of the discovery, and the inhabitants increased the precautions already in force against suspicious persons. A few days later a stranger was seen lurking in the undergrowth and a hunt was started, but the stranger evaded capture.

Shortly afterwards someone was again seen moving in the forest, and shots were fired, but again the stranger disappeared.

Some two weeks after the discovery of the parachute, an unknown man knocked at the door of a farmhouse. When the farmer opened the door, a tall, fair man who spoke in halting Estonian, asked him for food and shelter. The farmer was immediately suspicious, and at a sign from him a youth ran to the commune H.Q. and returned with some members of Self-Defence Corps who arrested the famished and exhausted stranger.

The man was not, however, a parachutist from beyond the River Narva [i.e. from Russia] but a rarer visitor; one, moreover, who had been well known in Tallinn before the war and who deserved a better fate than falling into the hands of the occupation forces. He was an Englishman, Ronald Seth, who had been teaching English in Tallinn University until the outbreak of war . . .

In his desire to do his utmost against Hitlerite Germany, he afterwards returned to Estonia as a parachutist . . . But the people to whom he came as a friend were expecting their enemies from a nearer front and could not know that this man from the skies was a herald of the 'third possibility' — Western intervention in the Baltic area . . . Thus he fell into German hands and of his subsequent fate nothing is known . . .

However, to return to my story, I shouldered the sack which I had dug up and set out for Kiiu Aabla. After an hour's walk through the forest I came upon the little house from the rear. The clouds had cleared away, and in the early morning sun and soft air of an Indian summer the cottage brought back many happy memories of our last holiday there.

Stealthily I made my way to the bathhouse which I found unchanged and still littered with hay. I went in, and through a chink between the log walls, I kept watch on the cottage, but saw no sign of life. Presently I heard footsteps coming down the path, and believing it might be Juhan, I had difficulty in preventing myself from going out to meet him. I was glad, however, that I had allowed discretion to prevail, for through my spy-hole I saw a woman, whom I recognised as Juhan's sister, unlock the door and go inside.

A moment later she came out again and crossed to the cow byre in a far corner of the paddock. I emerged from the bathhouse and a few seconds later I met her casually in the pathway.

'Is Juhan at home?' I asked.

She looked at me with the habitual shyness of a peasant in the presence of a stranger. Clearly she did not recognise me, though I had often sat in her kitchen chatting to her while she mended her husband's nets.

She shook her head.

'No,' she said, 'he has gone to the town.'

'When will he be back?' I asked.

I sensed her answer before she spoke, but it did not soften the blow.

'I don't know. Not for some days, anyway.'

Food was my most imperative need; but my experience of the previous evening had convinced me that I could not afford to take any more risks like that. Then I remembered that when we had been at the cottage in 1939 the latch of the kitchen window had been broken, so that the window could not be fastened. Knowing Juhan as well as I did, I was prepared to wager that the latch would still be in the same state. I went down to the kitchen window and gave it a pull; it opened and I climbed through.

The house was little altered inside. The piano accordion, covered with dust, lay in the corner of Juhan's room. The kitchen was still the untidy muddle that had been my wife's despair. I ransacked every pot, every shelf, every cupboard; but there was not a crumb to be found. No man, I imagined then, could fast completely for a week without dying of starvation. Although a week ago I had tipped the scales at twelve stone six, stripped, it was mostly muscle and bone. I am six foot one and a half inches tall and I had no reserve of fat to fall back upon. It was now Monday, and I had not eaten for forty hours, but I had deadened the hunger pains in my stomach by taking a morphia pill. I had a dozen left, and the same number of opium pills, but I could not go on like this. I should have to steal food whenever I could find it.

I went back into the forest, and, well hidden by the thicket, I made myself a comfortable bed of moss and pine needles and went to sleep.

It was dark and the moon had risen when I awoke. My intention was to try to procure some potatoes and a chicken, which I could bake in clay. (During my training I had been given an intensive course in poaching by one of the keepers on a famous estate.) I inspected the out-buildings of several cottages, but could find nothing. Not a potato or a feather was there, except at one of the holdings; but here, just as I was within a yard or two of the hut, a dog began to bark, then a hen cackled, so I retreated hastily.

Every day it was the same. The entire peninsula appeared to be devoid of food. I realised later that this was true of the whole country. What little the people had they kept in their houses, out of reach of neighbours who might come in the night. Most of the chickens had been eaten long ago by the Germans, and the cows too had all disappeared. Butter and milk had not been seen since the Wehrmacht had arrived.

This experience forced me to a decision. Until Juhan returned, I should have to exist on the few sweets and the whisky that still remained. I dared not approach these hungry, frightened people — not even Juhan's sister.

On the edge of the forest — which had become a symbol of safety for me now; as long as I stayed within it, I was sure I could not be caught — I counted out my provisions by the light of the moon. I had fourteen clear gums, six meat lozenges, a little more than a third of a pint of whisky, twelve opium pills and eleven of morphia. By rationing myself to two gums, one meat lozenge, one morphia or opium pill and three mouthfuls of whisky a day, I reckoned I could last for a week.

I knew the Germans would not easily give up the search for me and I decided that my best plan would be to keep moving under cover as much as possible. While I was settling down to sleep after my inspection of the cottage, a gun had been fired not far away towards the north; and on my way to the cottage I had heard aircraft warming up, then taking off, and had presently seen three Fieseler-Storch aircraft fly out to sea. So I knew that the German population of the peninsula was not inconsiderable. Besides, patrols of soldiers and forest guards, who might be in league with the Germans, were most probably on the look out for me.

Sleeping by day and moving by night seemed the safest plan. As I had slept all day, I now set out for the east coast of the peninsula. Next evening I struck back across the base of the triangle. So for the next six days, I wandered back and forth in a gigantic game of hide and seek.

The following Friday, 30th October, weakness was beginning seriously to hamper my movements. Seven days had passed since I had eaten proper food; at midday I finished my sweets, and in the evening my whisky. My speed was little more than a mile an hour and my physical condition compelled me to stop and rest every half-hour. But the temperature was still high and the air soft and spring-like.

All that night and the next one I wandered due east through the forest; then, having reached the eastern coast road again, I headed south. I followed the road fifty yards or so inside the forest, which here came right down to the edge of the road on either side. To be able to move more quickly and with less exhaustion I buried my siren suit and spade.

On Sunday the going was slower than ever. Besides feeling very weak, I began to have fits of dizziness. On Monday the weather changed, and the temperature dropped sharply. I could not get back to Kiiu Aabla by morning, so I looked about for shelter. I knew it would be too cold to sleep in the open next day.

As I stumbled along in the dark the ground suddenly disappeared under me and I found I was up to my waist in icy water. Half unconscious, I struggled out and staggered along towards the west coast road, which I reached at a point not far from where I had landed.

There was a curious half-light over the sea and silhouetted against it I saw about a hundred yards away a long, low hut. I did not know what it might contain but as it was only three or four yards from the edge of the sea I felt fairly certain that no one would be living there. Shielding my torch, I flashed it through one of the windows and saw inside a long table with knives and scraps of cabbage scattered about on it. Against the far wall stood some large tubs of sauerkraut.

The door of the hut was locked, but towards the opposite end on the seaward side, was another door leading to a separate compartment. I lifted the latch and went in. Flashing my torch round the walls, I saw at the far end a heap of cabbages reaching almost to the ceiling; against the back wall was a heap of hay. The rest of the hut was full of fishermen's gear and farmers' tools.

Closing the door behind me, I took off my soaked boots, sea-stockings and trousers and draped them on some nails in the wall, hoping they would dry before dawn, and that I should then be able to cross into the forest and perhaps get to Juhan's cottage. The time by my watch was half-past three. An hour or two's rest would probably restore my strength a little, so I clambered on to the hay and buried myself deep down in it. It was extremely cold and I felt very ill. During the day I had drunk some water from a stream and my empty stomach had taken violent exception to it. I had cut myself a slice from one of the raw cabbages, but before I had eaten more than a few mouthfuls I felt worse than ever and had to abandon it.

As I wriggled down into the hay to get warm I noticed a nauseating smell which seemed to come from somewhere underneath me. Pulling back the hay, I uncovered an untanned cowhide; it had obviously been hidden there from the Germans, who had a lien on all materials which could be put to any use.

Even if I had wished to sleep I could not have done so because of the spasmodic pains in my stomach. I lay there till seven o'clock, then decided to set out. But when I came to put on my sea-stockings and trousers I found them frozen as stiff as boards. However, I finally got them on to my numbed limbs and went out of the hut. As I turned the corner I saw an old fisherman coming towards me. He was not more than a hundred yards away, but he did not appear to have seen me, so I moved back quickly into the hut and once more buried myself under the hay.

Soon I heard a key in the lock and sounds of movement in the adjoining compartment. Presently the old man was joined by his wife, and together they began to prepare more sauerkraut.

I hoped that, being an elderly couple, they would not work for more than an hour or two; in any case I imagined they would presently make a break for food. I consoled myself with these thoughts until I remembered that it was broad daylight, and that however soon they went away, I could not emerge from my hiding place and cross the open country to the forest without great risk. So hour after hour I lay and listened to the old couple slicing their cabbages and to the occasional remarks they made.

After about an hour I heard footsteps outside my part of the hut. Then the door opened and the old woman pushed in a wheelbarrow which she began to fill with more cabbages. I lay there, hardly daring to breathe; but she suspected nothing, as I could tell by watching her through the hay. When the wheelbarrow was full she went out, closing the door behind her, and returned to her husband with her load. I realised that if they intended to work for long this was likely to happen several times. So I buried myself still deeper in the hay and went on waiting.

Several times the old woman came back and loaded her barrow, and before long there was an appreciable hole in the heap of cabbages.

About noon she went away, but presently came back with a bowl of soup. This I gathered from their conversation and the sound of drinking which came from the partition. Cramp now made it necessary for me to move; I had to do this with the greatest care, but while I was turning on to my back, my foot caught in a chair which fell with a clatter. Immediately there was silence. Then the old man said something, and in a moment I heard his wife coming along outside the hut. I sat up, intending to show her I was there and throw myself on her mercy; but the effort made me feel giddy and I fell back.

I heard the door open; the old woman came over and picked up the chair and put it back on top of the hay which covered me. Then, just as I imagined all was well, she stepped on something which caused her to lose her balance; to save herself she put out her hand, which rested on my knee, and pushed herself upright. She did not look to see what she had touched, but picked up a couple of cabbages and returned to her husband.

Thirteen times in all she came with her wheelbarrow, before dusk made it impossible for her to carry on any longer.

When they had gone I got up and stretched. My trousers,

stockings and underpants were still soaking, but there was nothing I could do about it; so I got back into the hay for the night. As I still had two opium pills left, I took one of them, which helped me to sleep fitfully until morning.

During the night the temperature again fell rapidly, and when I looked out of the hut at first light, there was snow on the ground. Winter had come, the northern winter, which would bring more and more snow, and falls in temperature until the thermometer touched minus thirty degrees. I felt dreadfully ill, and was sure that unless I could reach Juhan quickly I would eventually die of starvation. From my experience to date starving was a slow process and a very painful one. It was now Wednesday, 4th November: I had had no food for eleven days.

Thrusting caution aside I set out along the beach towards Kiiu Aabla. I proceeded jerkily, running a few yards, then pausing until I could co-ordinate my limbs for the next burst. Suddenly a blizzard came sweeping up and met me full in the face. After about a quarter of a mile I knew that until the weather improved I could not go on. I was very unwilling to give in, but when I came in sight of a small hay store, I climbed into it. I should explain that these hay stores were log-huts, about twenty feet by ten by ten, and were dotted about all over the countryside.

I knew that I could do nothing about drying my soaking pants and trousers, but I felt it would be wiser to take them off than to stay in them all day. It was now I discovered that the seams of my trousers had come undone. I had neither needle nor thread, so I tried to repair the damage with some string. But I was only partly successful, and thereafter I was always colder between my legs than anywhere else.

When I had settled myself I still felt very ill and my last pill did not help much. However I managed to doze, and when I looked out the following morning the blizzard had blown over. So I set out, determined to reach Juhan's cottage, praying fervently that this time he would be there.

I reached the cottage about half-past eight, and to my great relief saw signs of life. I knocked at the door, lifted the latch and almost fell inside. Juhan jumped up from his chair at the kitchen table, surprise mingled with fear in his face, until he realised who I was.

Through a swollen throat and cracked lips I croaked for bread. He pulled up a broken chair for me, and passed me a hunk of black bread that he was eating; then he drew a beaker of water from an enamel pail on a ledge near the oven; and so I ate the first solid food I had had for twelve days.

Juhan had changed very little, except that his face was thinner and his skin whiter. His smile still had its crooked appeal, and his shyness had not decreased. He did not ask where I had come from, or why, or what had happened, but only apologised for not being able to give me more to eat. The relief at finding him, of having someone to talk to, of feeling that here at least was someone who was not hunting me, was too much for my taut nerves and I burst into tears.

Presently he said: 'Have you come all the way from England to help us? That was brave, but I do not think there is much you can do. The people are sad and sick. Only a great army could stir them to great things.'

'It's not great things that I came to do,' I said. 'Anyway, I can do nothing now. I've lost everything.'

'You have come at a bad time, too. A fortnight ago the Russians dropped some parachutists in the forests near Tsitre. They haven't been caught yet and they have done a lot of damage. They blew up a gun on the Leetse head-land and killed a dozen Germans, and over the other side near Loksa they burnt some oil transports. Then three aeroplanes they keep in the forest to look for submarines have blown up mysteriously in the air. I haven't been here for a week. I've been trying to sell some sheepskins that I had put away. I need the money to buy flour and potatoes. I had the devil's own job getting back. There's a line of soldiers and Self-Defence men stretching from sea to sea above Tsitre. If I hadn't known one of the men, I wouldn't have got back.'

I smiled. I could have told him the truth about these incidents, though I had no proof. I explained to him what had happened to my equipment and he looked very grave. Then suddenly he motioned me to silence. There was the sound of a cart coming along the road.

'It's the patrol,' Juhan said. 'Come on, let's go to my sister's house. It's not safe here, we are too near the road, and the patrols pass every few hours. They're liable to search the place at any time. Besides, I have no food here.'

His sister's cottage stood farther back from the road, and one could approach it only by a rough track which separated the fields from the forest at the back of the house. Before we left we arranged a story to tell the others, according to which I had been on a British mission to Russia, and having been shot down on the way home, had been made a prisoner and taken to Riga. I had managed to escape from the prison camp, and with the help of friends in Riga, who had given me money and civilian clothes, I had reached Kiiu Aabla, after a journey lasting six weeks. I now wanted to get a boat and try to escape to Sweden.

When we arrived at Juhan's sister's house, she gave me some raw smoked fish, black bread, and a cup of barley coffee. It was all she had to offer. Food was almost non-existent, they told me, not just here, but everywhere in the country. Ever since the Russians came the people had starved.

'They have taken everything they could lay hands on. They've killed men, women and children, and deported a lot of others. If you went to Tallinn you wouldn't find a single one of your friends or pupils left there. Everyone who knew English at the University or attended the English schools has disappeared. Where they've gone we don't know, but sixty thousand of our people have simply vanished.'

'Then I must buy a boat to get away,' I answered. 'You must help me.'

Juhan shook his head.

'There isn't a single boat on the peninsula that's seaworthy enough to get you to Sweden. It's three hundred miles. In any case, you would never get by the naval patrol in the bay. The only hope is somehow to get you to Saaremaa. But that's easier said than done.'

Saaremaa is a large island, better known as Oesel, off the west coast of Estonia. Apparently the fishermen of Saaremaa were able to smuggle people through to Sweden.

Juhan's description of the morale of the people was totally unlike the Estonians as I had known them. In the days before the war they had been courageous and bold. Strengthened by seven centuries of suffering under foreign yokes, they had finally gained their independence, almost entirely by their own efforts, at the end of the first world war. That independence they had cherished, as only a people of spirit who had experienced slavery could have done. I could not believe what Juhan said of them now. If a nation can preserve its longing for freedom through seven hundred years of barbarity, it did not make sense to me that in a few short months the powerful determination which had helped them to survive so long could be completely obliterated. I told Juhan all this.

'Wait,' he said, 'I must fetch Denaki. He will convince you.' He went away to find his friend, whom I knew to have been a fairly influential man. After the Russian seizure he had fled from Tallinn and hidden near Kiiu Aabla disguised as a peasant.

While I was waiting, Juhan's niece, a woman of about thirty, came in. She refused my hand and did not smile. There was fear in her eyes.

'You must leave here quickly,' she said in German. 'Please! If they find you here we shall all be shot. Go — go now! Or give yourself up.'

'They will shoot me if I do that,' I said.

'Why should they? They are just. They do not shoot all Englishmen.'

'Very well, I'll go,' I said, trying to soothe her. 'But I must wait for your uncle.'

'It will do no good. Please go at once!' she pleaded.

Juhan came back with Denaki, who confirmed what Juhan had said; but he would not give up the possibility of my escape as easily as Juhan; he had an intellectual volatility that the shrewd peasant lacked. As we were discussing ways and means, the niece's daughter, a little girl of about seven, came running in.

'Mummy is bringing the soldiers to take the man,' she cried.

Denaki stepped quickly to the window. Beyond him I saw the woman and two German soldiers coming up the path from the road.

'Quick – the forest!' said Denaki.

The forest was immediately at the back of the house. I followed him outside and stumbled through the undergrowth until, overcome with weakness, I could go no further. I sank down on to the ground. My heels were now very sore and had been bleeding, for my stockings chafed them where the blood had dried.

The hopelessness of my position reasserted itself. For the first time the Germans now knew my whereabouts to within a few hundred yards. It would be impossible for me to make my way through the forest and evade even a half a dozen men if they were properly used. This was the end. I had really known all along that it would come to this, but with my habitual optimism I had refused to give up hope. But at last there was none left.

'I may as well get it over,' I said aloud.

I felt for my cyanide tablet. It was not there. I searched

all my pockets, but it was not in any of them. Then I remembered my Colt, which I had been carrying in my trousers' pocket because it made my armpit ache and I could not readjust the holster. I cocked it and holding it to my temple, began to say the Lord's Prayer. My finger tightened on the trigger, but the pressure seemed heavy. It refused to move. I lowered the gun and pulled hard on the trigger with both hands – a silly thing to do, because if it had gone off it would have given my position away, and there might not have been time to fire a second shot. I opened the gun and found the mechanism had rusted.

All of a sudden a new attack of dizziness came over me; my head swam and everything seemed to be going round. The next moment I was sick; the raw fish had been too much for my empty stomach.

Gradually the attack passed, and when my mind cleared I realised that if I could not kill myself the Germans would do it for me. I had forgotten my knife, but I do not think I should ever have had the courage to cut my throat. With the thought of a German firing squad doing for me what I could not do for myself, my resolution hardened. I would give myself up before they had a chance to capture me. But first I would have to get rid of my weapons, and any marks of identification that I might have.

I took off my holster, watch, gun, knife, flask and compass, and having wrapped them in my shirt, which bore Buenos Aires name-tabs, I buried them under a boulder. My silk maps and false identification papers I hid under another stone. Then came the problem of what to do with the money. If I hid it, it might never be found again.

The activity even of these few moments had tired me, not only physically but mentally, and it required an effort to make my mind function.

Hobbling painfully along, with acute pains now shooting up my legs, I made my way back to Juhan's sister's cottage. There was no one indoors except her husband, an old fisherman lying ill in bed. I found a scrap of paper and with a stub of pencil, wrote down my wife's name and address. I put this inside the waterproof bag and handed it to the old man, telling him what was in it, and that they could keep half the money if they would send the other half to my wife when the war was over and tell her what had happened. The old man nodded and I left him.

I went down the path on to the road and walked to what had formerly been the coastguard's cottage, but which I felt certain must now be a German post. When I got there, however, there was only a frightened woman who refused to answer my knocking, so I went away.

Further down the road I heard shouts and saw a boy running across the field towards me, pointing a rifle from his hip. He came to within a yard or two, then knelt down on one knee aiming the rifle point-blank. I stopped and put up my hands.

'Filthy Russian,' he said; he kept repeating it again and again.

Then suddenly I found myself surrounded by a crowd of men and boys and saw Juhan running towards me. Several of the men charged at me with their fists raised, cursing me for a Russian, and would have struck me, but Juhan shouted:

'He's not Russian! He's English! He's the English professor who was here in 'thirty-nine.'

At this they quietened down a little and looked rather shamefaced. But it was now too late. Two German soldiers came running up and marched me to their post, Juhan and one or two others following us.

CHAPTER 4

THE SECRET FIELD POLICE

I

THE field post to which I was taken was in a house not far from where I had landed. Juhan followed me into the lower room and told the sergeant the story we had concocted about my escape from Riga. I think he must have believed that he would be doing me a good turn. I knew, however, that a check would very quickly show that the story was not true. But if he could stick to it, it would probably be of use to himself, since if the Germans discovered that he knew I was a parachutist, and that he might be willing to help me, they would shoot him out of hand. Already his situation was extremely serious; for to succour an escaped prisoner of war was a capital crime. I was sorry for his sake that he had stayed by me for so long. It could do him no good.

Presently I was taken to an upstairs room and the sergeant, having sent the two soldiers who had accompanied us downstairs, took out a packet of cigarettes. He lit one and blew a cloud of smoke into my face. Watching me carefully, he said: 'You speak German, don't you?'

The phrase gave me a sudden inspiration. From now

on I would know no German. I gave him a puzzled look, as though I did not understand.

But he smiled and insisted, 'I think so.' Then, after a pause: 'I have a proposition to make to you. You have had no food, and you are hungry. No doubt you would also like a cigarette. Although it is against the regulations, I will give you some soup and bread and some cigarettes, if you will promise to say nothing about how you escaped. We are in the front line here, and discipline is strict. If our commander knew that we had surrounded you and yet allowed you to get away, we should spend many months in prison. We have reported that you disappeared before we could find you.'

I looked at him closely. He got up and walked round the table; I noticed as he did so that he had a slight limp. He put a hand on my shoulder.

'Well, *Herr Hauptmann*, is it a bargain?'

'All right,' I answered. 'But remember, I do not speak German.'

He nodded. 'Your parachute is buried in the field near the tree. They will ask you what you have done with it.'

'Are your men safe?' I asked.

'I've told them their lives depend on it,' he said.

He opened the door and called downstairs to an orderly to bring me some soup and bread, then motioned me to sit down at the table, while he stood over by the window.

46

'What did you hope to do?' he asked.

'I don't really know,' I said. 'One man can't do much against an army.'

'Not against a victorious army,' he amended.

The orderly brought in a bowl of thick soup, stiff with vegetables and chunks of meat, and a wedge of black bread. I ate ravenously. An Estonian youth of about sixteen sat on the bed with a rifle across his knees. Presently the sergeant went downstairs. Looking hard at the boy's Self-Defence Corps armband, I said to him:

'So you are a good Estonian; you work for the Germans.'

He flushed with embarrassment.

'Shut your mouth, dirty Englishman!' he muttered.

'I'm disgusted,' I answered.

He lifted the rifle to strike me, but at this moment the sergeant returned to give me a cigarette. A moment later the door was flung open and another soldier strode in. I did not recognise his badges of rank and did not stand up. The next moment he had snatched the cigarette from my lips and pushed me over backwards on to the floor.

'Stand up when a German is in the room!' he shouted. Then he turned angrily on the sergeant.

'Who gave him that cigarette?'

'I did, *Herr Oberfeldwebel*. He is an officer——'

'He's an English terrorist,' stormed the sergeant-major, but became suddenly calmer, as though the thought came

47

to him that to strike an officer, even one of the enemy, was a breach of discipline. He held out the cigarette to me, and told the boy to light it. I was still very weak and sick and was aching all over, but my mind was clear and active.

About three o'clock I was put into a peasant's cart, driven by a fat and genial corporal.

'You're lucky. This is the end of the war for you,' he kept saying. He was a man who obviously delighted in fleshly comforts, and to him the monotony of being a prisoner would have been preferable to the activity of a front-line soldier.

It was in the early dusk, about half-past four, that we drove into the courtyard of a farmhouse at Tsitre which had been taken over as the local headquarters. In a room lit by an oil-lamp I stood surrounded by German officers, one of whom was a colonel. But the organiser of the proceedings was a sergeant-major, who asked all the questions, and whom I came to know well later on. A swarthy man of middle height and about my own age, he was a Viennese called Nädlinger.

I was questioned first in Estonian and then in German, but speaking in English I said I did not understand. This seemed to make them angry, for it put me out of the ordinary run of agents and introduced just that touch of unorthodoxy which Germans fear and detest. From the beginning, therefore, I became a difficult case.

After about ten minutes of futile questioning, one of the officers began to speak to me in English. As soon as he did so, I realised the advantage I had unconsciously given myself, for I knew what the question was as soon as Nädlinger put it to him to translate, and while he was doing this I had a few precious seconds to formulate an answer.

'I am Major Vogl,' he said. 'If you tell us the truth we shall do you no harm. But you must tell us everything and it must be the truth.'

'I am quite willing to do that,' I answered. 'I was forced to come here by my superior officers. I did not want to come, but they made me. That is why I have given myself up.'

This answer caused a great commotion, and when there was silence again, Vogl asked a few more questions. Nädlinger, however, seemed to have heard enough to want to ask me further questions privately. Most of those present were not members of the Secret Field Police, in which he held the rank of sergeant-major.

Nädlinger having indicated that he had asked all that he wished to know for the moment, we divided into two parties, and I was taken back in a car to Juhan's cottage.

We burst into the kitchen by the back door, and found Juhan sitting with a friend looking at some snapshots of himself with my wife and children and me, which had been taken in 1939. They asked him how long I had been living in his cottage, why he had sheltered me, and what he had planned to do. But Juhan, with the guile of the peasant, put on an air of obstinate imbecility. Realising what they were up against, the party decided to move to the house of Juhan's sister.

She and her husband, having no oil, were sitting in their small kitchen in darkness. The old man was very frightened and began to whine miserably. After a time he produced the packet of dollars and krona, and, of course, the slip of paper with my wife's address on it. The old woman, however, showed great courage, and lashed the Germans with her tongue so viciously for bullying her husband that in exasperation the colonel ordered her to be taken into an adjoining room. But she had soon slipped back again, and now turned on me, damning me with every word she spoke. Was she not a pro-German? Had not two of her sons fled to Germany when the Russians came in 1940, and voluntarily joined the German Army? She had not helped me, beyond giving me a little food; and any woman who had a heart would have done that, seeing how exhausted I looked.

They now fetched the daughter from her house. Yes, she had brought the soldiers from the post. She had begged me to go and I had threatened to shoot her. (I remembered suddenly that while speaking to her I had changed my Colt from my trousers' pocket to the pocket of my storm-coat.) She did not like the English and had gone to the post at once.

After a few more questions, we got back into the cars, this time accompanied by Juhan and his weeping niece. An hour later we were driving into Tallinn, past the back of 9 Veizenberg'i tänav, where I had lived, past the English College, to the Market Place. In what triumph had I returned!

During the drive from Kiiu Aabla I had been wondering where they would take me. When we turned into the Uus Saadama tänav I knew the answer and groaned; for this way lay the Tallinna Keskvängimaja – the Central Prison – from which, even in our day, few were said to come out alive.

II

Nädlinger, who accompanied me with a corporal and another soldier, put his fingers to his nose as the inner gate of the prison opened to admit us. The stench that greeted us was the odour of centuries of filth. Supporting myself against the wall, I retched until I thought I had ruptured myself.

When my particulars had been recorded and Nädlinger had received a receipt for me, he told me that he would see me in the morning, and as he turned to go he gave me a military salute. I was led away through a series of bolted doors, down corridors where the air had condensed into something almost visible, past locked cells from which came shouts, laughter, singing and groans, and finally to the solitary confinement block.

I noticed the number on the door as the warder unlocked it to admit me – a small, discreet number painted in white: it was No. 13. As I stood blinking and looking round the tiny room, I suddenly realised that there was another occupant. He was lying on what served for a bed, and as I came in, he raised himself slowly on his elbow and looked at me.

He addressed me quietly in Russian, and when I shook my head, he tried Estonian, asking me who I was. I answered that I was an Englishman.

'And what are you doing here?' he asked in almost perfect English.

At this stage I was not sufficiently alert or I should have suspected all sorts of things; but I took him for what he said he was, and the memory of this lapse often made me smile later on when I came into contact with the highly organised 'Cloak and Dagger' department of Oflag 79.

'Do you mind if I have the bed tonight?' he asked, adding quietly, as if not wishing to rub salt into the wound of my new captivity, 'this is my last night.'

'Of course,' I answered, though privately thinking he was somewhat selfish. 'You are going out tomorrow?'

'In a way,' he replied. 'I am to be shot.'

The words swung me off the stool on which I was intending to sit and brought me round to face him. He looked no more than about nineteen.

'I am an agent,' he said. 'I was betrayed by the people I came to help. How about you?'

'I am an agent, too,' I said.

'And you were also betrayed?'

'In every nation there are a few people who are afraid of the enemy,' I answered. 'These people are my friends.'

'And how can that help you?'

'I don't know,' I said, 'but it may. The warders here are Estonians.'

'And they're afraid of the enemy, too, believe me. They'll promise you the earth if you say you'll tell them the truth. Tell them nothing, because even if you tell them everything, they'll kill you just the same.'

'So I have been told,' I said.

'Do you mind if we talk for a while?' he asked. 'I can't sleep.'

So for some time we talked. Young Russians, like the young Nazis were, are ardent political preachers when they have a bourgeois audience. I learnt more about Russia and Russia's aspirations that night than I ever knew before.

When Russia had won the war she would have to be recognised as a great Power, for she would improve her geographical position to such an extent that she would influence not only Europe but the whole world.

It must have been after midnight when at last the boy fell into a disturbed doze. I sat, miserable and shivering, trying to think how I should grapple with my situation. But my thoughts kept straying to the sleeping boy, temporarily happy in his oblivion. Gradually a resolution began to form itself in my mind, a burning determination that at all costs I would let my superiors, twelve hundred miles away in London, know what had happened; and particularly what this boy, Anton, had said. How I should do this I did not know at the moment; but from now on it was this desire that motivated the whole course of my conduct until I arrived face to face again with my superiors some two and a half years later. Having made this decision, I felt a little more settled, and with my head resting on my arms on the small cupboard top which served as a table, I slept from sheer exhaustion.

At half-past six we were awakened by shrill whistles in the passage outside. A moment later a broom and a dustpan were pushed through the hatch in the door. Anton took them and handed them to me.

'I've finished with work.' He smiled. 'From now on, I'm going to be lazy.'

A quarter of an hour later two hunks of black bread, each weighing about two or three ounces, and two mugs of hot water were handed through the hatch. We ate in silence. I wanted to say something to distract Anton's thoughts, but as the only remarks that came to mind seemed unutterably trite, I said nothing.

My feet were extremely painful, so I took off my boots and stockings to examine them. Besides the raw patches of flesh on both heels, my toes and insteps were beginning to swell and were turning green. Anton looked at them closely.

'That looks like frost-bite,' he said. 'You're in for a bad time. They won't do anything for you here. Your best plan will be to get your business over as quickly as possible, so they can put you out of your misery.'

As he spoke the light went out, and we rolled up the blackout. Through the whitewashed windows we could see the first light of dawn.

And then they came for him.

They manacled his hands and chained his feet. At the door, he turned to me, smiling:

'*Au revoir!* Keep your chin up. We shall meet again very soon.'

I heard his chains clanking along the passage, a key snapped in the lock, a door opened with a crash, then there was silence: a silence that one could feel, that one could touch. Then came the rattle of a machine-gun and in the passage a voice shouted an order.

For those of us who were left life moved on again.

III

At eight o'clock the warder opened my door and beckoned me to follow him. At the reception desk a German soldier with a rifle was waiting for me. He signed for me, and took me out.

We walked through the streets, which were dirty and unswept. The houses too looked broken down and filthy. Nailed to the door of every fourth house was a red notice which said *Ettevaatus tifus* – beware typhus. There were few people in the streets, but those few made me sadder than anything else, for their faces were white and pinched and their eyes sunken and afraid. As we approached they either drew back to the wall and stood against it until we had passed, or stepped into the gutter. Their clothing was threadbare and ragged, which it would never have been before the war. There were no cars, except for an occasional one carrying a German officer.

The trams were still running, but were reserved for German soldiers. Their destination boards now read Adolf Hitler Platz instead of Independence Square, Hermann Goering Strasse instead of Narva maantee, and Josef Goebbels Strasse instead of Tartu maantee. The great market place was empty. When I had last seen it, it had been packed, as it was for six days of the week, with stalls selling everything under the sun.

Our progress was slow because of my swollen feet, and we walked in silence, for I was in too much pain to talk. Besides, from now on I knew no German, so I could not ask where we were going. We had come into the Narva maantee, a long street stretching from the market place out of the town, and slowly we walked the full length of it, past the English College to the junction of Veizenberg'i tänav. We went up the bare, leafless avenue, where the blocks of flats revived intense memories.

As we approached No. 9 and turned in at the gate, I felt for a moment that I must be dreaming. Then it struck me that there was probably some ulterior motive in bringing me here. The coincidence was capped by our going into Flat 10, which had been my first home, now the radio headquarters of the Secret Field Police. Small things served as intimate reminders of my stay here. When presently I went into the bathroom I found the porcelain handle of the shower was still broken, and in the sitting room a large hook which I had put up above the divan to carry a heavily-framed print of Peterhouse, was still there.

Weak, hungry, and in pain, the old associations proved too much for me, and to the surprise of the headquarters' staff, I broke down and wept. When I explained why, they showed some genuine kindness, until the intrusion of a young officer.

So far I had had nothing to complain of, but this young man had about him an air of coldness and brutality. For several hours I was interrogated about my radio equipment. There was no point in my lying about it, since it was spread out on the table before me. When we reached the question of my transmitting frequencies I felt I had told them enough, and would say nothing beyond the fact that my five crystals had been marked A,B,C,D, and E. As they persisted, I began to have the impression that something had gone wrong, and when I refused to give way they tried to frame trick questions. But as this was ineffective, they began bullying. The lights were lit, and the blackout drawn.

Suddenly the young officer shouted at me: 'Where is your companion?'

I did not understand.

'My companion?' I said. 'I had no companion.'

'Five parachutes dropped from the aircraft,' he shouted. 'You'd better tell the truth.'

'But I am telling the truth,' I insisted. 'There was myself, three containers and the wireless package.'

'All right, we'd better leave that for the others,' said the officer. 'It's not a question for us.'

So they changed the subject to my radio code, leaving me puzzled.

When I first began my training, the radio codes which were being taught were rather complicated, and experience showed that young and often poorly educated foreigners found them too difficult to memorise. A simplified code was therefore introduced; but I kept to the more complicated one, which was harder to break; also its security checks, both true and false, made it apparent at once if the enemy tried to use it. Since I was the only member of the organisation using this code, I believed I should be doing no harm in divulging it, particularly if I did not reveal the true security check. In any case, it was obvious that I must have a code, and to have refused to give it would have endangered the plan which was already beginning to take shape in my mind.

When they had taken all this down, I was released for the day, and half-fainting, was led back to the prison. I had been given nothing to eat during the nine hours of interrogation, though my inquisitors had each had a container of soup and half a loaf of bread with some cheese. In my cell I found a bowl of cold, watery soup in which were floating two or three pieces of rotten black potato. I ate it, retching and weeping with hunger, pain and exhaustion. Then I covered myself with my single, threadbare blanket, and went to sleep.

IV

At the same time next morning the guard called for me again, and I shuffled painfully up the dirty street, past the electric station and the great flour mills of Puhk ja Pojad, both of which had been blown up by the Russians when they retreated from Tallinn in 1941. The Elektrijaam had been almost completely rebuilt and was working again, but the restoration of the flour mills was still continuing. After passing the burnt-out Ars Cinema, we turned right and a short street brought us to Aia tänav, which consisted of modern blocks, seven or eight storeys high. We went into No. 5 and climbed to the seventh floor.

Here I was greeted by Sergeant-Major Nädlinger, and since he had no English and I had no German, we talked in French. He spoke to me kindly, addressing me as *Herr Hauptmann*. He was alone in the flat, which served him both as office and living quarters. Having sent the guard away, he took me into the office and gave me a chair. First he asked me how I was faring in prison. I told him that I was getting used to the smell, but found the lack of food very trying. He then wanted to know how things were in England. But I was not deceived by his kindness, and I gave him a glowing picture of conditions and morale; which, incidentally, was not far from the truth.

On a large desk was a typewritten document which Nädlinger consulted from time to time, turning the pages and reading over questions half aloud. The few words that I caught made me anxious to see what the document was, though for the moment I did not see how this could be done.

'We are waiting for Major Vogl,' he said presently. 'He will be the interpreter.'

As he finished speaking the telephone rang and he jumped up to answer it. He seemed rather put out.

'I am here with the Englishman alone. I have no one else.' There was a pause. 'Very well, *Herr Major*, I will come at once.'

'I am called to another office to sign some papers,' he said, replacing the receiver. 'Will you give me your word of honour that you won't try to escape if I leave you alone? I shall lock you in, of course, and I shall be away only twenty minutes.'

I did not have to hesitate before giving the undertaking. We were on the seventh floor of a block of flats in the middle of the town, and short of picking the lock and walking out, I could see no way of escape. In any case, my feet would have prevented my getting far without being overtaken; so I gave my word.

He took me into his bedroom adjoining the office and told me to lie down and rest. He then locked the door leading into the passage-hall and pocketed the key, locking the double glass door which connected the two rooms.

He did the same to the outer office door and the entrance door.

As soon as I heard his jackboots clattering down the tiled staircase, I got off the bed and went to the window. A moment later I saw him hurrying down the street.

Examining the doors connecting the bedroom with the office, I noticed that the bolts on the doors were on my side. By drawing them and pushing outwards, the doors would open in spite of being locked, and I could see that with a little gentle manipulation I should be able to close them again and no one would be any the wiser.

In a few seconds I was standing by the desk in the office; but the document in which I was interested had gone. I did not think that Nädlinger would have taken it with him, but the drawers revealed nothing. The only other place in which to look was a cupboard, but it was locked. It was quite a light affair with plywood doors and a cheap lock, and in a very short time, with the help of a straightened paper-clip, I had it open. Nädlinger's document was on the top shelf.

It was a questionnaire for captured enemy agents, compiled by German Intelligence H.Q. and issued from Berlin. There were five or six closely-typed foolscap pages; a rapid reading of them, and of some pencilled notes in the margin, gave me a pretty good idea of the questions I should be asked. Notes on certain subjects about which confirmation was required also gave me a shrewd idea of how much the enemy already knew. I was shocked to find how extensive their knowledge really was. I knew that Major Larch and others in S.O.E. had been worried about certain equipment and codes being compromised, but I had not realised how serious the matter had become.

When I had replaced the papers, I found I was unable to re-lock the cupboard. I could only hope that Nädlinger would not remember that he had locked it before he went out. The glass door was easy enough to manage, and I was soon resting on the bed again, turning over in my mind what I should say.

During my last week with Major Larch we had discussed what I was to do if I were ever taken alive. We had thought out certain vague lines of action, one of which was for me to get access to a microphone. If I could do this, I could bring into use a second code which could be used either in broadcasts or letters; it involved a very difficult encoding process, but one which was absolutely unbreakable if it was well done. To bring this scheme off I should have to do two things: first, convince my captors that I was pro-German; second, appear to tell the truth, yet at the same time give as much misleading information as possible, so that if my first plan failed I should not have compromised the organisation too seriously, and might even succeed in confusing the enemy. Both propositions would obviously need very careful handling.

Clearly the line to take in connection with the first was to insist that I was both anti-Jewish and anti-Russian. If I could have had a few hours to work out a story, I thought, I might have a fair chance of success. But I did not know how long my questioning would take.

Presently I heard a key in the lock, and a moment later Nädlinger came in, accompanied by Major Vogl. We went into the office and the Major offered me a packet of ten cigarettes. I thought at first that this was part of the technique; but later, when I got to know him better, I realised that both he and Nädlinger were genuinely kind. Nädlinger took out his keys and went to the cupboard. My heart was in my mouth as I watched him fumble with the lock. To my relief, however, he opened the door and drew out the questionnaire.

Carefully he put some paper in the typewriter, then spoke to Vogl. Although I knew what he had said, when Vogl translated it I was no more convinced.

'If you will answer all our questions truthfully and fully,' said Vogl, 'we can promise that you will not be shot and will arrange for you to be sent to a camp until the end of the war. If you try to mislead us, however – and we shall know at once – it will be very unpleasant for you.'

On that understanding my questioning began. It was a complicated process. Nädlinger would consult his directive, read the question out to Vogl in German, Vogl would write it down in English, write down my answer in English, and translate it into German for Nädlinger to type. The advantage to me of this system was that as soon as Nädlinger read the question in German I was already framing the answer in my mind. The respite that Vogl's careful translating and writing gave me was of inestimable value.

It was a searching questionnaire and was based on the Nazi doctrine: '*Ist deine Grossmutter in Ordnung?*' – 'Is your grandmother in order?': 'in order' meaning Aryan. My statement was written by Nädlinger in narrative form, and when it was completed it ran to fifty-six typewritten, single-spaced, foolscap pages. I remember this, because I had to initial each one.

I began by giving a detailed account of my life and career up to the time I had joined the R.A.F. Except that I said I had been conscripted, all that I said up to this point was true. Now, however, I began to mingle fact and fiction, to suit the plan that I had devised. I continued with an account that was only partly true, of my service in the R.A.F., stressing my non-combatant duties. From then on I gave my imagination free play, and this is the story I told:

One day at the beginning of March 1942, I was instructed by my Commanding Officer to report to a Mr Goldman at an address in London, at 14.00 hours the following day. I asked my C.O. if he knew what it was about, but he could tell me nothing.

I reported as instructed, and found Goldman to be a small Jewish-looking man with a large nose and thin grey hair brushed back. We talked in general terms about Tallinn. The Air Ministry authorities knew I had been there, because when I was commissioned I had had to fill in a form indicating what languages I spoke and which foreign countries I had been to.

At the end of about half an hour Goldman indicated that the interview was closed. I asked him what had been the purpose of it, but he replied that he could not tell me at the moment, though I should be hearing from him again.

A few days later I was instructed to report to him once more. This time I found him with another man, to whom I was not introduced, and who did not speak throughout the interview. Goldman came at once to the point. He said that he understood the oil plant at Kohtla Järve was producing three hundred tons of oil a day, and that he wanted me to find out whether this was true, and if so, what was happening to it. I was the only Englishman of suitable age who could speak the language and knew the country.

I protested at once that although I might be of suitable age, I was not at all suitable in other respects. I was a student, not a man of action, and, moreover, I was married and had two small children. I could not possibly consider such a proposition.

This made Goldman very angry. He began to talk about country and honour coming before family in times of war. Again I refused and got up to go. As I went out, he shouted after me, 'I think you will do this!'

Four days went by, and I was then instructed to report to a Wing-Commander Beeding at the Air Ministry. When I arrived the Wing-Commander began to threaten me.

'Your refusal is a disgrace to the Service, and I have to tell you that unless you withdraw it, you will be reduced to the ranks.'

This would have been a serious thing for me, since my children were at school, where I was paying five pounds a week for them. We had no home, having lost everything in Tallinn, and in England had twice been bombed out. But perhaps most serious of all would have been the disgrace this would have been to my family. When I returned to my post that evening, I wrote to Goldman accepting.

Towards the end of the month I was told to report to Major Beech (this was the name I had decided to give Larch) on April 5th. When I saw him I was made to sign various papers, including a declaration given under the Official Secrets Act. He then outlined my operation, which, besides sending home information about the oil plant at Kohtla Järve, would entail the carrying out of active and passive resistance, and the transmission of military information. I was to pay particular attention to events on the nearest part of the Russian front.

I followed all this with a long and detailed account, still mixing truth and falsehood, of my training, without of course, making any mention of S.O.E. I said I had been instructed in the use of explosives, wireless, codes and so on, and had been taught how to organise passive resistance groups, and about the organisation of the German forces.

Besides myself, there were students of all nationalities, including five French, three Dutch, two Norwegians and one Czech – all officers. In the garden of the house where we had been trained there was a large lake, well stocked with fish. I used to fish there every evening, and as the Commandant was also a keen fisherman, I became very friendly with him. He told me a great deal about the organisation, which he ought never to have revealed. He said that it was financed by Jews and industrialists, who had large financial interests abroad. He thought that the man Goldman probably had important interests in the Kohtla Järve oil plant.

From here I went on to talk about the course I had taken in parachute jumping, and then of my return to

London and my last interview with Major Beech, in which we had settled the final details of my operation. While I had been at the various schools Beech had come to see me from time to time. More than once I had told him that the operation would fail because I did not speak Estonian sufficiently well to impersonate a native successfully. Beech had finally said to me, 'If I were you, I should not refer to this again. The authorities believe you are deliberately pretending you don't know the language.'

As my training progressed I became more and more convinced that I was virtually committing suicide. I had been told that I could not be provided either with identity papers or local money, since the Russians, who could have provided both, would not do so, the Russian Secret Service being at loggerheads with the British, and on this particular point considered Estonia to be within their own sphere of interest. Major Beech warned me, therefore, that I must be on my guard against Russian agents as much as against the Germans. I also became more and more convinced that I was being used solely as the tool of Jewish industrialists.

For this reason I had decided that I would carry out the mission up to the point of landing, but that immediately I had landed I would surrender to the Germans.

Still drawing considerably on my imagination, I then described the period between the beginning of October

and the night the operation started – October 24th.
According to my version, it had been decided that I was
to be dropped on the coast, not far from Port Kunda. On
being told to get ready for the jump, I had looked out
and seen that we were not over the dropping point, for
below me there were three small pensinsulas, whereas
Port Kunda was a single headland. This I tried to convey
to the Squadron-Leader, but he shouted back something
which sounded like 'petrol'. I concluded that the aircraft
was running short of fuel, and that although we were a
hundred kilometres from our objective, I must jump now,
as not to have done so would have been a breach of military discipline, in my refusing to obey the order of a senior
officer.

I made a bad exit from the aircraft and lost sight of my
equipment coming down. When I landed, I buried my
parachute, and then began to look round for my containers.
But I could not find them, and at the end of ten minutes,
gave up the search. Then I heard a dog barking and voices
along the road. I lost my nerve. The propaganda with
which we had been soaked at the 'waiting-school' was still
very fresh in my mind, and I was terribly afraid of being
tortured.

I ended by describing the rest of my adventures more
or less accurately; how I had at last made my way to
Juhan's house and had asked for his help, and how, when

I finally realised that the game was up, I had tried un-successfully to shoot myself, and had then surrendered.

V

In presenting my story in this form I had three aims: first and foremost, to remain alive; secondly, to ingratiate myself with the Germans, win their confidence, and convince them that, although I had been caught red-handed, I was not an ordinary spy; third to insinuate into their minds the idea that my broadcasting ability was not unimportant.

In appearing to give my interrogators as much 'information' as they believed I could give, I had to be careful not to betray any important details about the organisation or its personalities. There was no point in lying about my previous activities in Estonia, because I realised it was quite possible that all my documents might still be in the University archives; besides, Juhan's niece had told the Germans my name and the positions I had held at Tallinn.

My story about being forced into the organisation will no doubt seem very naive, but I was not unversed in German psychology, of which I had made a fairly close study, and was convinced that this was the approach which would appeal most to the Nazis. I might get into difficulties if I came up against a real soldier, who might not be a one hundred per cent Nazi; but that I should have to risk.

I had imagined that this interrogation by Nädlinger was to be a preliminary enquiry, and that at a later date I should be tried by court-martial. I expected, therefore, to have time to invent embellishments for my story which would clinch it. I had had so little opportunity to work out its ramifications that I knew there must be minor flaws; but I felt that if these were attacked by a prosecutor, I might be able to bluff my way out by pleading a faulty memory. In the meantime, by going over the various points I should probably recognise their weaknesses and be able to prepare my answers accordingly.

Throughout my statement I had followed a mnemonic scheme, particularly with regard to names. Major Larch, for instance, I had renamed Beech, and for other officers I took men from schools that I had not described, transplanted them, named them mnemonically, and gave composite descriptions.

It took us several days to complete the statement, and I was more than a little worried about the hundreds of details I had made up on the spur of the moment to fit the various questions. Though I knew that I should certainly be asked to repeat much of what I said, and that this would be minutely checked, I thought I had over-stepped the limits even of my rather phenomenal memory.

By this time the state of my frost-bitten feet was reaching its climax. The prison doctors could do nothing for me, beyond giving me a chit that allowed me to lie on my bed during the day. The pain was so intense that it was only with a vast effort and under the spur of questioning that I could get my mind to function at all. When I returned each evening to my cell, my mind simply refused to work, and I wallowed in the pain almost as though it were a luxury, letting it flood my senses.

During the last afternoon of my interrogation two other officers joined us. When we had at last finished and I had signed and initialled each page of my statement, they went into an adjoining room for a discussion with Vogl and Nädlinger, leaving me alone in the office. A few moments after they had gone, I saw lying on the table, the pad on which Vogl had recorded my answers in English before translating them to Nädlinger. Without waiting to consider what the consequences might be, I picked up the pad and stuffed it into the top of one of my sea-stockings. I was never searched on returning to prison, and I think this must have tended to make me over-confident.

Presently they returned, and I had my first uneasy moment. Vogl came directly to the table and began searching for something. But he said nothing, and whether it was the block he was looking for, or whether he guessed where it might be, I do not know. I smuggled it successfully into the prison, and in the following month, I committed all my answers to memory, and there they still are.

On the second or third afternoon of my interrogation, I was again questioned about my transmitting frequencies by the radio officer, the cold and rather brutal young man, who, since Vogl was not available, had brought his own interpreter. I recognised the latter as soon as I saw him. In 1938 I had bought a German Telefunken radio, which gave a much better short-wave performance than British models. This man had sold me the set, instructed me in its use and had installed it in the Veizenberg'i flat. He spoke Estonian without any accent and had an Estonian name. It appeared, however, that he was not even a Baltic German, but a Reich German, who for several years before the war had been a Nazi agent.

I now discovered that besides speaking flawless Estonian, he spoke English far too well for it to have been learned at school. I said to him that I could not see why they were asking me about the frequencies. They had the crystals, and experts would soon be able to analyse them.

'The ruddy crystals aren't in the radio package,' he explained. 'And they aren't in the two containers, either. The third one was only found today, and some bastards had practically emptied it. All there was in it were a spade, some heavy rubber gloves and some rubber pads.'

I knew that these things had been in the odds-and-ends container, but where the crystals were, I could not think. They should have been in the radio package. When I mentioned this point to Military Intelligence on my return, the subject was changed with an abruptness that conveyed its meaning unequivocally – at least to me. Clearly someone had omitted to include them in the package; an oversight which it was too late to remedy by the time it was discovered.

Although I did not wish to hurry the suggestion about my broadcasting, I felt that I ought to begin to let the idea filter into the minds of my captors. I therefore asked for permission to make a personal statement. This being given, I wrote, in general terms, that I would be prepared to work in any way against the Russians and the Jewish industrialists, and mentioned that I had had experience of counter-propaganda and was a skilled broadcaster.

When I had finished, Vogl and Nädlinger bade me *au revoir*, promising that they would do all they could to help me. Nädlinger came to the door and pressed a parcel into my hand, telling the guard who was to take me back to prison that the prison authorities were to allow me to have it.

In my cell I uncovered half a loaf of stale black bread. It was as hard as wood, but I ate it all, and for once I lay down satisfied.

CHAPTER 5

TALLINN CENTRAL PRISON

BEFORE the war, the Tallinn Central Prison had accommodated political prisoners and the worst types of criminal. It ranked as the third or fourth worst prison in Europe, after such notorious institutions as the Cherche Midi in Paris and the Moabit in Berlin. The conditions under which the prisoners lived were such as to eliminate all self-respect within a few weeks. The quality of self-respect is the most important factor in a prisoner's character, if he is not to deteriorate into a member of some sub-species.

Conditions of living were now even worse than before the war. Prisoners were herded together, thirty or forty at a time, in rooms which, under healthy standards, might have held a dozen. One lavatory, actually within the room, served this number; and one, or in exceptional cases two, small sinks with a cold water tap were the only washing facilities. There were no beds, and the only covering was a stinking, threadbare blanket.

The numbers were much inflated at this time. The solitary confinement block was being used for prisoners on remand awaiting trial as political criminals, or as foreign agents, and for condemned prisoners under sentence of death. There were fourteen cells on each of the three floors, and in these forty-two cells there was a daily average of seventy-six prisoners. I was able to keep a personal check on the numbers in the block, because before the rising-whistles blew the orderlies counted out the slabs of breakfast bread near my cell.

Men and women – generally two or three men to one woman – shared a cell meant originally to hold one person. This was a German measure to quieten prisoners, who, unless they were of some importance, waited many months for a trial.

When I had been there for some weeks a young peasant girl was brought to my cell by a German soldier with a message from Nädlinger.

'Would you like this girl to make a home for you?' I was asked. 'The *Oberfeldwebel* thought you might like company. You can keep her for yourself.'

I spoke to the girl, who told me that her name was Eva Kass and that she had been parachuted by the Russians over Narva. She was calm, but there was in her eyes the fierce flame of the fanatical patriot. Apart from the rather odd morality of the situation, I did not wish to be closely immured with a tigress, so I asked the soldier to thank the *Herr Oberfeldwebel* for his consideration, but said that I preferred to be alone. The soldier looked at me in astonishment.

'But her medical card is clean,' he protested.

'Nevertheless, I prefer to be alone,' I said.

I was to discover later that the satisfaction of sexual appetite was a subject very near to the German heart. The Gestapo questioned me for several hours about the provision made for it in the strictly segregated training schools of the 'Organisation', and were frankly cynical when I said that the question never arose.

The warders in the Tallinn Central Prison were Estonians, either elderly men or youths who ought still to have been at school. They treated us roughly, which I do not suppose was their fault, for they looked pinched and unhappy, as though they too had suffered and were suffering still. They were worse when a German was at hand, being then sycophantic towards their masters and brutal towards their charges.

Cell 13 was a small room about twelve feet by eight by ten, which contained a water-closet, one half of a tall heating oven – the other half projected into the next cell – a sink with a cold tap, and a low cupboard in which I kept my bowl and spoon; the top of this cupboard also acted either as a table or a stool. On a metal frame fixed to the wall was stretched some torn sacking which served as a bed; on it was a sack of chaff for a mattress and one blanket stiff with filth and reeking of the dirt of former users. The window, though large, was so thickly whitewashed that one could not see through it; nor could it be opened, and there was no ventilator. From the door to the cupboard under the window measured nine feet; this was my exercising space.

Winter descends with a dramatic suddenness in Estonia, just as spring suddenly arrives without any previous announcement. Outside, the temperature had again fallen very sharply. Indoors it can have been only a few degrees higher, since we had no heating, except for a few hours after midday on Sundays. As the top part of the oven heated more quickly than the lower, I used to stand on my stool, draped in my blanket, and lean my cheeks and hands against the warm tiles. This was strictly against the regulations, but after a vivid passage with one of the elderly warders, during which I reviled him, perhaps rather unfairly, I was left to my own devices.

As there was no fuel for heating, there was no hot water for baths or shaves. The soap ration was fifteen grammes, or about half an ounce, a month – a sliver of ersatz, fatless, blue-grained hardness which would not lather. This allowed one to make a pretence of washing one's face once a day, but the hands had to be cleaned by rubbing them together under cold water from the tap. No change of underclothes was provided, and for more than three months I wore the clothes in which I had landed. After the first month I began to smell so badly that I noticed it myself.

Our diet, which was very simple, was hardly sufficient to sustain life. At seven o'clock a mug of hot water and a two-ounce slab of coarse black bread were thrust through the hatch in the door; to be followed four hours later by a pint of hot water in which floated four or five pieces of bad potato or else a half-dozen pieces of macaroni or a cabbage leaf. I can remember my delirious excitement when one day I counted no less than ten small pieces of macaroni in my soup. At three o'clock four small potatoes were distributed, but these were so weevil-eaten and frost-bitten that you were lucky if you could find one that could be eaten. After this there was a break of sixteen hours, until seven o'clock the next morning.

The whistles blew reveille at half-past six, and a quarter of an hour later roll-call was taken. About nine o'clock a senior warder inspected the cells, after which there was nothing to do for nine hours, until evening roll-call at six o'clock and lights-out – for all except the prisoners under sentence of death. Thus, for twelve hours a day there was practically nothing for a prisoner to do except sit and think.

To enliven the monotony, two or three times a week there would be a rattling of chains, a clanking of doors, and the sound of jokes and laughter as heavy feet went down the corridors. For a little while, until we heard the splutter of a machine-gun in the courtyard below our windows, life seemed to be suspended. For the first few weeks these frequent executions affected my morale, and for at least an hour afterwards I would sit on my stool with my teeth chattering, praying incoherently. It was not really fear but a feeling of impotence, a kind of feverish rage that pervaded my thoughts, so that I was unable to control myself or see reason. I think it was the laughing and joking that did it. I could not understand how courage of that kind could be destroyed if there was a God in Heaven. After a time I realised that I was weakening myself physically by allowing my senses to be played upon in this way, and as I was daily awaiting a summons to a court-martial, at which I should need the use of all my wits, I should have to pull myself together.

I can recall exactly the moment when the decision to control my behaviour entered my mind. It came almost with a click, as though a lobe of my brain had been flicked over. From that moment a streak of ruthlessness, of which I was hitherto unaware, entered my nature and has remained characteristic of me ever since.

In the days immediately following the end of my interrogation, my frost-bite reached its climax. My feet were causing me such agony that it was impossible for me to stifle my moans. All day long I sat on the stool rocking backwards and forwards, tears streaming down my cheeks. I could not get my boots on, and to put my feet to the ground paralysed me. One day a young warder took pity on me and saw that I was taken to the hospital block. How I made the journey I do not know; I have no recollection of it. But there the Estonian doctors laughed, in spite of themselves, when I asked them to do something for me.

'All our medicines and ointments have been taken by our "friends",' they said. 'All we can do is stand by and watch people die.'

During this period I was quite unable to concentrate on learning Major Vogl's notes, and this worried me because I was expecting at any moment to be court-martialled. As the days went by, however, and there was no summons, my feet started to mend, and gradually I began to settle down to a routine of solitude. Except for the senior warder at morning and evening roll-calls, I saw no man's face and I spoke no word to anyone. Three times a day, after I had learned Vogl's notes, I repeated all the answers. The rest of the time I spent with my own thoughts.

To be shut up with one's thoughts for thirteen hours a day, with nothing to occupy one's hands, is an experience which can do no one any good. It is a state which must in time become insupportable, unless one has a natural urge for meditation or an extensive intellectual background. Neither of these qualifications were very highly developed in me, but I had lived a full life with extremely little leisure, and now I welcomed the opportunity to apply certain philosophical remedies to my own case. I had a fairly extensive knowledge of English literature and knew by heart long passages from Shakespeare, the whole of Milton's *Comus*, and a good deal of Browning, Shelley, Keats, Donne and Coleridge.

With these resources to support me, I settled down to a routine of complete inactivity; it was prevented from becoming monotonous only by physical pain. I could not accustom myself to the lack of food, and at one time the pangs of hunger overcame me. For toilet paper I was supplied with old newspapers, and on this occasion, unable to bear the pangs any longer, I ate some of it. Within a few hours I was attacked with violent diarrhoea, which persisted for several days and reduced me, in my weakened state, to the point of collapse.

Not long after this, the A.D.C. to the Town Commandant came to inspect the prison on behalf of his august master. I had not met the Town Commandant, but I feel sure he could not have excelled the splendour of his representative, who brought with him a glitter of youthful perfection, both sartorially and in his deportment. He was only a flight-lieutenant, or rather, its German equivalent, but his uniform would have outshone that of a captain of the Household Cavalry. His delicate nose was creased at the end in a permanent wrinkle, and a rimless eyeglass tapped against the buttons of his tunic.

He strode into Cell 13, glanced round quickly, then stared fixedly at me for some moments. At last, in perfect Estonian and without any trace of accent – a fact so striking that I felt he must be a native – he asked, 'Have you any complaints?'

Momentarily off my guard, and still weak from the effects of my newspaper feast, I replied in Estonian, 'I am hungry. Please could I have another piece of bread every day?'

He did not answer at once, but continued to stare with a look of contempt spreading over his features. With deliberate care he fixed the eyeglass in his eye, then said with a sneer, 'And why should we feed a dying man?' Then he turned abruptly, went out, and the door was slammed.

I stood staring at it for some moments, and then sank down on my stool and wept tears of chagrin and self-pity at being betrayed by my physical weakness into becoming vulnerable to a Nazi snub. When I had recovered I determined to overcome my hunger and never again to let it get the better of me.

Shortly after this incident I had a day out. I was taken by Nädlinger and Vogl to look for my gun, shirt and knife which I had hidden under the boulder not far from Juhan's sister's cottage. When I had been asked if I would be able to find them, I had said 'Yes,' never imagining they would be wanted. It was essential that these things should not be found, since buried with them were my forged identity papers and my silk operational maps.

The scenes of desolation in the city found their counterpart in the countryside. The thing that struck me was how few people we saw on the way. Perhaps they hurried indoors when they heard us approaching, for only the Germans possessed motor-cars. But the peasants' cottages, heavily-thatched, low, log huts, had a completely deserted air. No smoke came from the chimneys, and there were no chickens or animals to be seen. The flat, wide country with its isolated clumps of silver birches was a dead and silent land under a thin layer of snow. All along the Narva Road from Tallinn to Kiiu Aabla were single graves or small groups raised in mounds at the roadside. On each grave was a rough wooden cross and the steel helmet of the dead German who rested there.

At a cross-roads where we turned off stood a gibbet, from which hung the bodies of three partisans. Theirs had been a slow death, for their heads hung forward, not twisted round in the awkward attitude of a broken neck. I thanked providence that I was a soldier and that if I had to face an executioner, he would be wielding a rifle, not a rope.

When we came to the forest at the back of the cottage the snow had so changed its aspect that I could quite honestly say that I could not identify the place. For almost two hours, Nädlinger, Vogl and I paced up and down in the forest, prodding and searching under stones in a glade which I knew was not where I had hidden my equipment, for it had had an immense boulder in the middle of it. At the end of two hours, Nädlinger gave it up, and we went back to Tallinn with him not in the best of humours.

A couple of days later I left my cell again. But when I reported to the reception desk, my former Wehrmacht acquaintances were not there to sign for me. Instead, two civilians helped me down to a waiting motor-car, for the walk in the Kolga forest had caused my feet to swell again and I was unable to tie my boot laces.

We drove to the Toompea, or Dome Hill, as the Estonians call it, a plateau with steep sides, one of which is a sheer precipice, that dominates the city. On this hill the viceroy of King Valdemar, the Danish king who conquered Estonia in 1218, built a fortress, the main tower of which still stands. Later conquerors added to or replaced the Danish fortifications, and the existing fortress dates from the first half of the seventeenth century. Later still the Hansa merchants of Tallinn – which was once a Hansa port – built their houses there, and these were afterwards converted into government offices.

We drew up before one of these offices and I was half-carried up the steps and into a room on the ground floor. One of my guards stayed with me while the other went into an inner room. Neither of them had spoken a word to me or to each other, and I was too conscious of the pain in my feet to provoke conversation.

Presently I was summoned to the inner office, where two men were seated behind a desk. When they spoke they did so in excellent English, but with a German accent. The Estonians, whose language is full of open vowel sounds, speak English without any trace of an accent. The German, on the other hand, unless he has been educated extensively in England, speaks our language with a gutteral roughness.

'We have brought you here,' the spokesman said, 'because we wish to ask you a few questions about your radio equipment. We know that you have said you do not know your transmitting frequencies; but the transmitter is of such a type that the frequency numbers must be known, otherwise the transmitter cannot be tuned. Now, it will be much easier for you if you will tell us than if we have to compel you.'

Swaying from the pain in my feet, I answered that I had never known the frequencies; there was a light-system which indicated when the transmitter was tuned in.

'You are very foolish,' said the other man. 'If we must compel you, it will be very painful.'

Again I insisted that I did not know, but with a gesture of impatience the first speaker threw down his pencil.

'Don't let us waste time. Take him away,' he exclaimed.

The two guards dragged me out of the office, across a corridor and into another room. The furniture in it was simple. Placed obliquely across one corner was a bare table with a chair behind it. Facing one wall was a large, gilt-framed mirror, and opposite this a high-backed armchair on a platform, which allowed the chair to be swivelled round. Behind this chair was a powerful standard lamp with a bowl reflector.

I was thrust into the chair and my arms and legs were then strapped to it so tightly that the straps cut into my flesh. A wide band which was fixed to the chair-back was placed round my forehead, pulling back my head so that I could not turn it. When I was thus secured one of the two men I had seen in the other room came in and sat down at the table. The two guards took up their positions behind me.

The man at the table put on a pair of dark spectacles, gave a nod, and immediately the light behind me was switched on and its glare, reflected in the mirror, struck me full in the face. Instinctively I closed my eyes; but immediately I received a blow across my nose and mouth and a warning that every time I closed my eyes I should be struck.

The glare seemed to sear my eyeballs. In a silence broken only by my grunts of pain, I heard the inquisitor say: 'You see, we mean business. Now, tell me, what were your frequency numbers?'

'I don't know,' I answered. 'I am telling you the truth.'

'What were your frequency numbers?'

When I did not answer, one of the men behind me gave me another blow across the jaw.

'Leave him,' the inquisitor ordered in German. Then, turning to me: 'Your numbers?' He went on repeating every few seconds in a flat, monotonous voice: 'Your numbers? . . . your numbers? . . . your numbers? . . .'

Whenever I shut my eyes, a sharp blow reminded me to keep them open. Sometimes I cried out that I did not know the numbers. Sometimes I cried out simply from pain.

Presently the voice changed, and I realised that my inquisitor had been replaced by someone else. The new man insisted on my answering every question, till at last I began to mutter in a slow rhythm: 'I don't know . . . I don't know . . .'

I soon began to sweat and could feel the moisture trickling down my face. After a while the first voice returned and ordered me to stop chanting.

'You had five crystals?' he asked.

'Yes, I had five crystals.'

'Why five? Three would have been sufficient.'

'I had three crystals. I said so in my statement.'

'Just now you said you had five.'

'I made a mistake.'

'How many did you have?'

'Three!'

'But you first said you had five. Had you five?'

'Yes, I had five.'

'You had five. What were your numbers?'

Having got me out of my rhythm of denial, he returned to the old question: 'Your numbers? . . . your numbers? . . . your numbers? . . .'

Presently the voice changed again, and now, accompanying it, I heard the clicking of a metronome.

'Your num . . . bers? . . . your num . . . bers? . . . your num . . . bers? . . .'

Presently I lapsed into unconsciousness. When I came to I was soaked from head to foot with ice-cold water. There was some conversation in German between the guards and the inquisitor, who wanted to know if I was all right. Then the voice and the metronome began again.

The pain had now become a dull ache suffusing every part of my body. At this stage there was a pause. The arc lamp was put out, but its glare seemed to have imprinted itself on my retina. I heard men moving about the room, then I became aware of a smell of fried bacon, onions and potatoes. For a long time there was silence; gradually the light died from my eyes, and as the smell continued my mouth was flooded with saliva which dribbled through my lips and ran down my chin. The nerves of my stomach began to jump convulsively. Then I heard the first voice saying: 'You are very hungry?'

'By God, I am!' I answered.

'You have been hungry for a long time? You could eat some beautiful bacon and some steak and onions?'

'Yes.'

'They smell very good, don't they?'

'They do indeed.'

'You would enjoy eating them, isn't it?'

'God, yes!'

'They are there before you – you can see them. There is enough there for four men to eat. You could do with it?'

'Yes.'

My mind had not yet lost its hold on the situation. I knew still that this was part of the torture. I tried to think of other things, but the smell of the food was in my nostrils.

'You may have that plate and all that is on it, if you will tell us your numbers.'

I paused, tempted as surely only St Anthony can have been tempted. Then I shouted violently, 'I don't know them! All your tortures can't make me tell what I don't know.'

'You damn fool!' the man shouted back. 'We are many against you. We will *make* you tell.'

I had rattled him, and the knowledge made me less despairing. If it had not been for the pain, I think I should have smiled.

'*Licht!*' snapped the inquisitor.

The light came on again, a great searing sun; my senses reeled from the shock: so it began all over again. Time and again I fainted, and each time came round drenched with ice-cold water.

I lost all count of time. My lips swelled from the constant blows, so that I could hardly move them to give my answers, which were always the same: 'I don't know . . . I don't know.'

Hours must have passed – hours that seemed like a waking nightmare; and I knew that after all I would have to utter the little words that would release me. What were they? I searched the corners of my mind. 'Seventy-four point . . . ?'

I worked my mouth, but before the words came to my tongue the support was taken from my head, and with a stab of pain which momentarily numbed what was left of my senses, my chin fell forward on my chest, the straps were taken from my arms and legs, and I slid to the floor. A moment later I felt myself being pulled upright and the blood began to flow through my limbs again; but I could see nothing but dancing red, blue and green lights.

I recognised the voice of the first inquisitor saying, with a yawn, 'What's the time?'

One of the men holding me replied, 'Half-past two.'

The clock of the Dome church had been chiming nine o'clock as we had gone up the steps into the house. Only five hours: yet it had seemed like five years.

They took me back to the prison in a car and half carried me upstairs to the reception desk. When they had left, and the warder ordered me to go before him to my quarters, I had to ask him for his hand. Who he was I don't know, but my state seemed to arouse some tenderness in him.

'Why did you come, Härra Professor?' he asked. 'Our sons who could have helped you are gone. You suffer now in vain.'

'Not in vain,' I answered. 'I've kept faith with them; and that means a lot to me.'

'And to us. But what good is faith without sight?'

'I don't know. But now that I am blind, perhaps I shall find out.'

He said nothing, but gripped my hand tightly. When he had unlocked the door into my corridor, he said to the floor warder:

'The prisoner is blind. Help him.'

'Blind?'

The voice I heard was not the voice I had expected.

It was the night warder who spoke. 'Is it night?' I asked in halting German.

'Yes, it's night,' replied the old man.

My questioning had lasted not five hours but seventeen!

Next morning a doctor came to me in my cell. But beyond bathing my swollen face with warm water and putting a bandage over my eyes, he could do nothing for me. Gradually the impression of dancing lights faded; but it was three weeks before I saw men again, and for some time they appeared only as walking shapes.

A day or two after the bandages had been removed from my eyes, I was asleep in bed when I was suddenly awakened by the door being flung open and a little old man was thrust violently into my cell. He was dressed in rags with a sheepskin coat over a Russian shirt and tattered trousers bound round with rags and straw which also protected his feet. His matted hair hung about his shoulders and drops of moisture glittered in his beard, while the smell of him rivalled my own stench.

He sat down on the stool, blinking at me, and gabbling in a language which I recognised as the patois of the Setud, the peasant inhabitants of Petseri, the south-east province of Estonia. When I could break in upon him, I spoke in Estonian, and he replied fluently but with such a broken accent that I had difficulty in understanding him.

'Who are you?' he asked after a while.

'I am an English officer,' I said.

With a cry of *'Angliski!'* he threw his arms about my neck and embraced me on both cheeks, our beards caressing one another. His name was Matsve Konjovalev.

A stream of questions followed. Why was I here? How had I been captured? Was I going to be shot? Had the Germans tortured me? Was the torture bad? Did they pull the finger and toe-nails out? I must hold out my hands to let him see. We talked for a time, until the warder came round and warned us to keep quiet.

It was terribly cold, but I knew that tomorrow we should be comforted for a few hours when the oven was lit. Matsve lay down on the floor, curled up in his sheepskin coat, and was soon asleep and snoring. And how he snored! I stood it as long as I could, then I leaned over and jabbed him in the ribs. He grunted, and changed his position, and then for some time was silent. Next day he was very quiet. Reaction had set in, and fear was in his eyes. By persistent questioning I drew his story out of him. He had been accused of helping Russian parachutists; but it was not true.

'What will my little Alexandrina do to feed the little ones?' Matsve wept. Then he cried out loudly: 'Oh Holy Mother and St Joseph, take me out of this place and let me go back to Petseri! I will walk all the way.'

My heart bled for the poor little man, who had no understanding of what was happening, except that for some reason he had been separated from his wife and family, and that without him they would have even more difficulty in surviving than they had in the present harsh times.

'Will they let me go soon, do you think?' he asked.

I could not tell him that he would never go back to Petseri; that he would either face a firing squad or be sent to a labour camp to work until his body was so broken that it could no longer house his soul.

'They will let you go in a day or two,' I said, with as much conviction as I could manage.

He sat on the stool shivering, looking at me now and again with the pleading eyes of an animal seeking friendship. That night, and for the rest of the time that he was with me, I gave him the bed and took the thin palliasse and the blanket, with which I contrived to make myself as comfortable on the bare floor as my protruding bones would allow. My frostbite troubled me very little by this time, but my hunger caused me a deeper and more restless anguish.

On Monday, shortly after breakfast, they took him out. He went away, frightened and eager to please. When he returned late in the afternoon – the blackout had already been drawn – he fell into my arms. I laid him on the bed and put the folded blanket under his head. The warder, who was peering through the spy-hole, lowered the hatch to order him off the bed, but I spoke so sharply that the man said no more and sheepishly withdrew.

There was a long gash over Matsve's eye and another on his cheekbone from which the blood was still trickling into his beard. I bathed his face with the rag that served me as a towel and did what else I could to comfort him, till his cries subsided and he began to mutter in his own strange language. Suddenly he got up, fell on his knees by the bed and began praying aloud, invoking in constant succession all the saints in the Orthodox calendar.

I could stand it no longer and swore at him in English. He stopped and lay down on the bed again, where he remained muttering from time to time, his body shaken by spasmodic fits of trembling. Eventually he fell asleep, and I curled up on the floor and went to sleep too.

I don't know how long I had been asleep, but presently I was awakened by an unusual noise. I sat up and saw that Matsve was not on the bed. Then I saw that his body was hanging from the pipe leading into the closet cistern. Perhaps it would have been more humane to have let him hang there, but I did not think of it. I jumped up, yelling for the warder, and lifted Matsve's frail body so that its weight was taken off the strap by which he was hanging.

Eternity seemed to pass before the warder came, bleary-eyed with sleep. In a flash, when he saw what was happening, he was wide awake. He was a young man, not much more than a boy, and only two nights before had replaced the usual night warder who had gone sick. Obviously he was not yet accustomed to staying awake at night. He took his knife and cut Matsve down. I laid the old man on the floor and felt his heart: it was still beating feebly, so I turned him over on to his stomach and began artificial respiration.

The boy began to whimper. 'Will he live? They'll shoot me if he dies.'

'Why weren't you doing your duty?' I said. 'If you hadn't been asleep he couldn't have done this.'

While I worked I was thinking. Why should I not demand a *quid pro quo* for Matsve's life, which at this moment was in my hands? This was a chance that might never come again.

'If I save him,' I said to the boy, 'I shan't tell anyone. But in return I shall expect you to do something for me.'

He promised. 'Anything but food,' he added. 'They search us for food every time we come on duty. You must save him though. For God's sake save him!'

He was talking so loudly that I had to remind him there would be little good in my saving the old man if the other guards were attracted by his noise or if someone should overhear us. I thought this last warning might be effect-ive, though I did not know whether the stool-pigeon system would operate in such distant and relatively un-important areas. At once he dropped his voice to a whisper.

'What do you want?' he asked. 'I can't bring food.'

'I don't want food,' I answered. 'Tomorrow night when you come on duty, bring me a pencil and some sheets of paper.'

The mention of pencil and paper upset him almost as much as food.

'You're not supposed to write,' he faltered.

'I know, you fool!' I replied harshly. 'Well?'

I took my aching arms from Matsve's back. 'All right, I don't go on,' I said.

'Very well, I'll bring it,' he almost shouted.

'Remember,' I warned him, 'if you don't, I shall tell the Germans all that has happened. The bruises round his throat will be there for some time.'

'I promise,' he whispered.

I worked on, and in a short while Matsve came to. He muttered something that I didn't catch: perhaps he im-agined himself to be already in Paradise. I wrapped him in the blanket and my storm-jacket and made the boy bring his own greatcoat, telling him the old man might still die of shock if he was not kept warm.

For the rest of the night I sat wide awake on the floor,

huddled against the cold oven with my teeth chattering. I was thoroughly selfish in my attitude towards the incident, for next day Matsve was every moment in terror that the previous day's experiences might be repeated and moaned continually, 'Why did you not let me die?' But I shut my ears and planned what I should do.

When he was not reproaching me, he spent the time on his knees, praying aloud to the Holy Mother, St Joseph, St James and a multitude of other saints, defying the warders who time after time lowered the hatch and shouted to him to stop. But today I did not mind. I sat preparing in my mind the letters I would write.

That evening after Matsve had begun to snore, the cell door opened quietly and the young warder came in. With a great show of caution he pulled the door to and drew from his pocket a pencil and some narrow slips of paper.

'If they are found——' he began.

'They won't be found,' I assured him. 'Even if they are, I won't tell where I got them.'

He looked far from happy, but said nothing.

That night, and for the next five nights, I wrote a series of eleven letters to my wife, in which I incorporated in my letter-code, which I had not disclosed to any of my interviewers, brief details of what had happened. During the day I sat on the stool and dozed.

The day came when they fetched Matsve and shackled

his hands and feet. He knew why they had come, and now that the time had arrived it seemed as though some inner strength had transformed him from a cringing, timorous old man into a hero. At the door of the cell he turned to me and said:

'I am going where I shan't be beaten or be weary any more. Good luck, *Angliski*.'

He was not alone. Eighteen others were lined up in the corridor and went out with him. Before the machine-gun's clatter cut the cord of our suspense, we heard strong voices chanting the *Internationale*.

When I had finished my letters I made them into a small packet and wrote on the outside: 'Will the finder please send to: Mrs R. Seth, 5 Wickham's Place, Keswick, Cumberland, England.'

Ostensibly to mend a tear in my blanket, I obtained from the warder a needle and thread and sewed the letters into one of the inside pockets of my storm-jacket, doing the job so well that it was impossible to tell where the opening was. Whether the letters would ever get through, either during the war or after, would depend entirely on my luck. I certainly believed that I ran no risk in carrying them or that there would be any danger if they were ever discovered. Difficult though the code was to operate, I felt pleased with my efforts, for the letters read quite naturally. Whatever happened now, I had done my best to let my superiors know where I had got to and had tried to pass on the information which I had picked up on the way.

On December 21st I was taken down to the prison offices, where two German soldiers, a sergeant and a corporal were waiting for me. The sergeant spoke English with an accent he must have picked up within the sound of Bow bells. His friendliness was embarrassing as he took my fingerprints and measured and weighed me. I weighed eight stone thirteen pounds, which was a loss of three and a half stone in the two months since I had left England. I wondered what was the point of it all, unless I were being used as an experiment. I could see no harm in asking, but before he replied there was a pause. Then he said: 'They've told you, have they?'

'They've told me nothing,' I said.

The corporal asked in German what I wanted, and then if the sergeant intended to tell me.

'They didn't say not to,' the sergeant answered.

'Then tell him. It's kinder,' urged the other.

The sergeant suddenly became very busy with his papers.

'On Wednesday you are to be hanged,' he said at length. There was no feeling in me of weakness nor any recoil or fear, only a welling-up of anger.

'I'm to be hanged!' I exclaimed, my voice loud with rage. 'But I haven't had a trial!'

I knew that when a prisoner has been condemned the light is left burning in his cell throughout the night, so that the warders may be sure he does not cheat the gallows under cover of darkness. My light had never been out since long before Matsve Konjovalev had joined me, so I ought to have realised long ago that I was a condemned man; but the thought had never occurred to me because I had had no trial or any chance to speak in my own defence.

'I'm sorry, Captain,' the sergeant said, putting his hand on my shoulder. 'I never thought I should string up an Englishman. But if I refused they'd find someone else and string me up alongside you. But I'll see it's over quickly. That I can do. Don't hold it against me.'

'I understand,' I said.

CHAPTER 6

THE GALLOWS CHEAT

I

BACK in my cell my rage subsided, and I told myself that what was happening was really what I had been expecting. A trial would have done me no good. I had been taken in civilian clothes, so there was no defence. Now that I knew what was to happen, and what was more important, when it was to happen, a kind of serenity came upon me. I had before me forty hours of life: forty hours in which to make peace with God and myself.

As the time passed I found that I had no doubts at all about God's understanding of man's sins and weaknesses, and with this realisation my feelings of fear disappeared. I had no inclination to lobby my Maker, and most of my thoughts during these hours were not centred on God but on my family. Nor was my sleep disturbed. The routine of the prison ticked by. The so-called meals came round; inspection and roll-call took their usual turns; and when night came I slept until the bread-ration for our wing was delivered in the hour before reveille.

After I had woken it seemed hours before they came for me. I was still physically weak and walked a little unsteadily down the corridors and into the prison yard, where an escort of soldiers in steel helmets and greatcoats trailing almost on the ground was waiting for me. We paused at the desk, where one of the soldiers signed for my body, then he led me to the middle of the escort. An order was shouted and my last march to the Baltijaamplats began.

Dirty, frozen snow crunched underfoot. Tallinn looked more disconsolate and unhappy than ever and the people more cowed. Yet I noticed that the few men we met raised their hats as we passed and two women with shawls over their heads fell on their knees and crossed themselves. Their gestures of respect were gestures of defiance to their conquerors. One or two German soldiers whom we met looked away.

Where the Suur Patarei meets the Saadama tänav we were held up by a road-block. An ill-shod horse drawing a heavy cart had slipped and fallen between the shafts. While we stood waiting for the road to be cleared, a little lean and hungry dog came sniffing round my legs. The odour from my body had grown worse during the last weeks, and having taken one sniff, he sprang off, his tail between his legs, and sat down on the edge of the pave-ment, baying at Death.

We now quickened our pace to make up for the time we had lost, and the hands of the station clock stood at three minutes to ten as we came into the square; a

perfect example of German timing. The clock struck
ten, and it quickly became obvious that the schedule
had been upset. A train ran into the station, and presently
people began to emerge into the square. Again I noticed
the men lifting their hats and one or two German officers saluted; but they did not stop.

Slowly the seconds dragged by. I began to shiver with
cold – cold that brought with it the beginning of fear,
which began to lick with little flames at my heart.

I glanced round, stamping my feet in a pitiful attempt
to stop my shivering, and for the first time noticed the scaffold, a platform raised on trestles with uprights at each end
supporting a cross-bar; from the middle of this bar dangled
a rope at the end of which was a noose. I calculated that
the platform was about three and a half feet above the
ground and about five feet wide. From beneath the platform, on the right-hand side, protruded a metal bar.

My glance went back to the clock. We had been waiting
six minutes, for the hands now stood at three minutes past
ten. Never has time passed more slowly for me. I began
to wish that it could all be got over quickly. Unless something happened soon I might make an exhibition of myself
not at all in the best traditions of the English martyrs.

Presently a car hooted impatiently, and a few seconds
later drove rapidly into the square and drew up. From it
emerged in great haste a Wehrmacht captain and my two

acquaintances, the executioner and his assistant. The whole scene sprang to life, and incongruously the R.A.F. aphorism, 'Wait and then hustle', passed through my mind. I remember feeling cheered by the knowledge that in the super-organised German Army the same thing applied.

The captain and the others rapped out orders in quick succession. I was lifted on to the platform and the sergeant pinioned my arms, while the corporal strapped my feet.

'I don't like this, captain,' said the sergeant, who kept up a sort of running commentary. 'Sorry I've got to do it. But it won't hurt. It'll be over before . . .'

He held a bandage to my eyes.

I shook my head. 'Is that necessary?'

'Rather see where you're going, eh? O.K.'

Down in the snow a voice was reciting in badly-spoken Estonian. I saw that a little crowd had gathered a few yards beyond the ring of soldiers round the scaffold, as though compelled by curiosity to stand and watch. The sergeant had some difficulty in fixing the noose over my head because I had not had a haircut since the beginning of October. Then he jumped down from the platform.

I watched him march smartly up to the captain and salute, then heard him shout at the full expansion of his lungs: '*Alles in Ordnung!*'

Even now I don't think I had any real belief that in a very few seconds I should be dead. I was still perfectly well aware of what was going on. Another order was shouted. The escort and guards clicked their heels loudly and made a noise with their rifles. I could feel the rope chafing the skin of my throat as my pinioned body swayed. The captain turned about and faced me squarely. His face was grim and his bearing correct and soldierly as he saluted me. Simultaneously with his hand touching his cap, I heard a clatter of metal. The trap on which I was standing suddenly gave beneath my feet, fell a few inches and then stuck.

I heard shouts, and saw blurred figures running hither and thither. Then I fell forward. The rope tightened behind my ears, and my eyes were filled with bright lights and then darkness.

II

It was early in the afternoon when I came to and found myself back in Cell 13. My neck was stiff and bruised. I eased myself off the bed and with my legs trembling violently, I staggered to the door and knocked. The warder lowered the hatch and peered through.

'What's happening?' I asked.

'I know nothing,' he answered. 'But don't worry.'

I tried to draw him out, but could get nothing more from him.

Someone had been thoughtful enough to fill my bowl with soup, and it now stood on the cupboard top, cold and uninviting, a thin watery liquid with a leaf or two of sour cabbage floating in it. Nevertheless, I drank it and began to feel slightly refreshed.

I lay down on the bed again, believing that I was sufficiently an object of curiosity to flout the rules. It occurred to me that my position must be unique, for I must surely be the only German victim who had cheated the gallows at the very last second. The warder seemed to agree with me, for though he was continually lowering the hatch and peering in, he made no attempt to move me from the bed.

It was cold in the cell, and I began to shake all over, partly from the shock and partly because of the temperature. So I rolled myself up like a dog in my stinking blanket, and when I had got over my trembling I fell asleep.

When I awoke the light was on. So soundly had I slept that I had not even heard them come in to fix the blackout. On the table were four small frost-blackened potatoes and a mug of water that had a layer of ice on it.

I was now less shaky when I stood up, and as I perched on the stool and peeled the potatoes, the hatch was lowered and I saw the face of the young night warder regarding me.

'You all right?' he whispered.

'Yes, thanks,' I said. 'Come in.'

He unlocked the door quietly and came in, pulling it to behind him. Except for the warder on the floor above, who would most probably be dozing, there was little chance of our being disturbed, for the noise of the door leading into the other wing would give sufficient warning.

'Have you heard what happened?' I asked.

'Only rumours. Still, there must be some truth in them. They put the scaffold up yesterday afternoon and left a guard on it, but they drank some vodka during the night, to warm themselves up, and didn't keep a proper watch. Some of our people screwed a couple of slats underneath the trap, so when it was supposed to fall it just stuck. When the crowd saw there was something gone wrong this morning they began jeering and the officer thought it was going to be a demonstration and they might try to rescue you, so he brought you back to prison. You were to be a warning to us not to trust in the Third Possibility – what we're not supposed to talk about. You were to be left hanging over the holidays.'

'And what's to happen now?' I asked.

'One of our old men says they won't try again till the New Year holiday.'

I had nothing to say, and for a moment there was silence. Then the boy asked: 'Why did you come?'

Immediately the suspicion flashed into my mind that he might be an *agent provocateur* and that it might all be an elaborate trick. But then I dismissed the idea; there could be no point in it. Hadn't I been caught red-handed?

Then when I looked up I saw real sympathy in his eyes, which I had not seen in any man's since I had come here. So I said:

'I came because I promised that I would.'

'But what good did you hope to do?'

'I came to help your people. We could have done something: every little helps.'

'We're too far away,' he said. 'And the Russians are worse than the Germans.'

At this moment we heard steps coming down from the floor above, and he left me hurriedly.

When he had gone I began to think about the New Year, and suddenly my nerve snapped. The day's experience must have affected me more than I had realised. Recollecting it, I did not think I should be able to go through it again without breaking down.

I slept little during the night because of attacks of sobbing which I could not control. Only by the most determined effort was I able to prevent myself from making some violent and foolhardy attempt to escape.

In the afternoon I began to feel a little less sorry for myself, for as well as the usual frost-bitten potatoes, each prisoner was given a pint of hot oatmeal porridge as a gift from the Governor. I can taste it all these years afterwards. I do not believe that anything I shall ever eat again will be so delectable as that unsweetened, unsalted oatmeal. It was the first change in our diet, the first new taste we had had since I arrived.

During the afternoon the hatch in my door was lowered and a book was thrust through by an unknown hand. It was not a book I should have chosen. It was in French and its title was *Des Nuits Orientales de l'Amour Erotique*; not a very suitable book, one would have thought, for those in prison. However, it was certainly a distraction for my mind, and proved a little later on to be indirectly of the greatest importance in my affairs.

In the evening, the young warder came with some more details. He had been to the Nazi organisation, of which he was a member, and had heard that the captain, the sergeant, the corporal and four guards had all been shot after an inquiry by the local commander. They had been charged with a serious dereliction of duty in not having examined the scaffold before the execution. The captain and his party had been late in arriving because someone had forgotten to obtain signatures to certain papers until just before the time fixed for the execution. The captain had given as his excuse for abandoning it the fear that there might have been an attempt at rescue.

Whether there had been a plot the young warder did not know. It is difficult to imagine what the perpetrators could hope to do in a country overrun by a whole German Army. They could not have got me away without some delay, and that would have meant that sooner or later I must be caught again. Yet if there was no rescue plot, it is equally difficult to imagine what they hoped to do, unless they were merely making a gesture of defiance; though for all they knew such a gesture might do me nothing but harm. It was a gesture that demanded courage, the traditional courage of the Estonian; an unselfish gesture that must have completely disregarded the terrible reprisals which would surely follow. All the same, the action proved more successful for me than its instigators could ever have hoped. I often wonder whether it was luck or through some higher agency that the captain forgot to obtain the signature he needed. My life had been saved by an administrative slip. Had it not happened, the wooden slats would have been discovered, and not only would I have died, but the attempt would have been fraught with terrible consequences for those who had taken part in it.

On Christmas morning I was reading *L'Amour Erotique* when I found between its pages a piece of rice-paper. While I was trying to spin out my Christmas dinner, consisting of a pint of sauerkraut soup, as long as possible, I had a sudden inspiration. I tore off a piece of the rice-paper about the size of a cigarette paper, and with a stub of pencil which I had hidden in the cistern of the water-closet I wrote:

On and after April 10th, 1943, listen on 'A' frequency at 17.00 hrs. GMT and 23.00 hrs. GMT. Listen but do not reply.

I rubbed the paper in the dust on top of the cistern, screwed it up and pushed it well down into the pocket of my storm-jacket.

When the senior warder came into my cell on his tour of inspection on Boxing Day, I asked him to get in touch with the German authorities immediately, as I had some very important information for them. I think he thought I was trying to save my neck by turning traitor at last, for he gave me a look that was full of scorn and reproach. However, he agreed to do as I asked.

I hoped that when the Germans discovered what I wanted to tell them, I should be taken before the highest officers in Tallinn, the men who had condemned me to death without trial. If I could manage to get to them, I intended to impress upon them that I was willing to do absolutely anything to revenge myself on the Jews and Bolsheviks who were responsible for my present circumstances. Perhaps I could get them to put me in front of a microphone, or could work my way into a situation in which I could somehow pass on my information. I was sure that if I could speak to the German authorities, I could convince them that I was sincere.

The following day I waited on tenterhooks, telling myself over and over again that if only I could create the right opportunity, I could still turn defeat into some small success; but nothing happened. When the senior warder visited me the next morning I remonstrated with him, insisting that my information was vital and would not wait. Perhaps he was trying to save me from myself, but he merely shrugged his shoulders without a word and went away.

For the next two days I was extremely depressed. The idea which had previously buoyed up my spirits became a millstone around my neck. Long periods of these days are completely blank in my mind, and I really think I must have gone mad. In the periods that I remember I jabbered to myself, wept loudly, banging and kicking the walls and door. Eventually the day warder brought a doctor who gave me some medicine and told me to lie down. Although I felt physically a little calmer, I was still greatly distressed in my mind.

About ten o'clock on December 29th the warder came and took me to the reception desk, where two soldiers were waiting for me. A car was standing in the courtyard and together the three of us drove to Aia tänav, where, to my surprise, I saw Nädlinger standing on the kerb. The soldiers got out, and Nädlinger took their place. Without any preamble, he said: 'We are going to Riga.'

115

CHAPTER 7

A REPRIEVE

As we drove along Nädlinger explained what had happened. An hour or two after I ought to have been dangling on the scaffold, orders had arrived from the General Officer Commanding the Baltic front for me to be taken to Riga for further questioning. But the order had been delayed by a breakdown in communications.

This was even better than I had hoped. Any officer at General Headquarters was far better for my purpose than the highest ranking local officer.

'Did you get my message from the prison?' I asked.

Nädlinger shook his head. No message had been sent. I was now convinced that the senior warder must have decided that I was turning traitor.

Nädlinger treated me quite kindly. Indeed, in all my contacts with him he had never been anything but quiet, efficient and understanding. He did not handcuff me or shackle me, and now when he saw how weak I was he did not make me hurry. He also handed me a parcel containing half a stale loaf of black bread and a packet of ten cigarettes, a gift from Major Vogl.

We arrived at Tallinn airport five minutes before the

aircraft was due to leave. The airport, when I knew it, had always been beautifully kept, smart in appearance and up-to-date in its equipment. Now it looked a shambles. The tarmac was flaking from the runways, which were scarred with bomb craters, and the grass was worn and rutted.

Out on the runway was a familiar sight – an old green-painted Junkers 52, coughing and spluttering and shaking in every rivet and spar. It looked – though it obviously was not – the same old aircraft that Lufthansa had run on the Berlin-Helsinki line before the war, in which, en route for Tallinn, I had sometimes carried the British diplomatic bag to the Legation in Finland. I never made the trip without some trepidation, for more than once aircraft had been known to disintegrate over the Gulf of Finland and had never been seen again.

Nädlinger seemed not at all at ease.

'Have you flown often?' I asked.

He grinned sheepishly. 'This is my first flight.'

We must have looked an ill-assorted pair. No attempt had been made to tidy me up for my public appearance. It was nearly three months since I had washed; my clothes were tattered and I stank horribly. My red beard flowed freely and my hair was curling over the back of my collar. The prosperous-looking German businessmen, with their secretaries or 'friends', stared at me in surprise. If they had known that I was an enemy agent under sentence of death, their astonishment might have been even greater.

Poor Nädlinger! As the journey progressed he became as sick as anyone I have ever seen travelling by air. We must have appeared increasingly odd as the time passed – the tattered, filthy beggar supporting an N.C.O. of the impeccable German Army.

After an hour's flying we touched down at Riga airport. Green and staggering, Nädlinger was pathetic in his attempt to be dignified as he handed me over to two Luftwaffe corporals who had come to meet us.

We boarded an army truck and drove through the snowy streets of Riga to the prison. Although under the influence of war Riga looked decidedly changed, it did not seem so drab, nor its people so tired, as Tallinn. The Germans were adopting a policy of wooing the Latvians and there was much less atmosphere of repression than in Estonia, where the Master Race policy was being carried out ruthlessly.

The prison, which had been taken over by the *Kriegswehrmachtshaftanstalt* – literally, War Forces Arrest Prison – had been built by Peter the Great in 1725. It was a T-shaped building, the lateral part forming the administrative and staff quarters, and the stem divided into two long halls placed end to end. On either side of the first hall were fourteen cells on each of the two floors. A gallery, approached by a spiral staircase rising from the centre of the ground floor, formed a platform outside the cells on the upper tier. One guard was on duty on the ground floor, and another at the top of the staircase. These individual cells housed prisoners on remand who were awaiting trial.

In the second hall there were no cells but on each floor there was a big dormitory for prisoners serving sentences of not more than three months.

I was put into Number 10, the 'casual' cell, in the first hall on the ground floor. Compared with my Estonian cell, it was a dilapidated hole, though the atmosphere was fresh and healthy; a pleasant change from the Augean reek of the Tallinna Keskvängimaja. The floor and walls, which had once been white, were now filthy and the floor was smeared with dried excreta. The bed consisted of bare boards raised about two feet off the concrete floor. There was no blanket, no pillow and no table, except for a broken wooden flap which was screwed to the wall.

There was, however, a radiator, as in all the other cells. The boilers were in the basement and were looked after by a number of Jews. The glass in the window was clear, and through it I could see the sky and the leaves of an evergreen shrub, both of which brought me joy. For the lesser calls of nature I was provided with a stinking tin, which leaked; for the rest, one knocked at the door until the warder came and escorted one to the lavatory.

I was not happy in these surroundings, but knew from experience that it was merely a matter of adjustment. To help myself to become accustomed, I listened intently to all the new sounds. There was much more doing here than in the Tallinn prison and I did not feel so cut off, particularly in the evening when the sounds of the staff's radio and of their piano and songs came through from their quarters. My worst time was at night. My body was so thin that when I lay down on my bare wooden bed, I very quickly became so numbed all down one side, that I would have to turn over to get to sleep again.

My fellow prisoners were young Germans from the Luftwaffe, the Army and the Navy, and there were also conscripts of all nationalities. We were allowed in the wash-place five at a time, and although we were not supposed to talk to one another, we did. One morning a young Norwegian airman, who had noticed that I was keeping my trousers up with a piece of cord, pushed a leather belt into my hand. When I got back to my cell I found scratched on the inner side, *Dux Femina Facti* and 'Good Luck England'. I was intrigued by the Latin inscription, meaning 'A woman was the leader of the exploit,' and diverted myself for some time by inventing versions of what might have happened.

They all knew I was English, for my name and nationality were chalked on a board nailed to the cell door. At meal-times we had to queue up with our bowls in the centre of the hall and file past the cook, and as my cell was near the serving table, all the prisoners were able to read the board. My extraordinary appearance raised a lot of curiosity, not only among the prisoners but among the staff, who made a point of visiting me at least once during each tour of duty.

We were on German Army rations and after the diet which I had received in Tallinn, the meals were like banquets. At seven o'clock we had four ounces of black bread and jam and a mug of coffee substitute. At eleven-thirty we had lunch, consisting of a pint and a half of delicious thick soup, at the making of which the Germans are past-masters; a different variety was served to us each day. At five o'clock we got four ounces of bread, a little fat, and some cheese, sausage or fish. Occasionally we had two hard-boiled eggs and a mug of coffee or tea substitute. During my stay here I also received two lemons.

Number 10 was next door to the cook's. When the food was brought in, the cell doors were unlocked, mine being the first. While the guard was opening the others, the cook, a fat, middle-aged man who was serving four years for attempted desertion, and who was horrified by my appearance, would slip me an extra two rounds of bread and jam. Whenever there was a surplus of soup, sausage or cheese, he generally persuaded the guard to come to me first (though strict rotation was the rule), using as his argument for thus befriending me that it was good propaganda for the Party.

The Commandant of the prison was a Wehrmacht captain who was never seen, and was rarely on the premises. The executive responsibility was vested in a sergeant-major and three sergeants. The sergeant-major was a strict disciplinarian, and treated me in the same way as the rest of the prisoners. The other three, however, went out of their way to show me kindness and consideration. If the sergeant-major was not supervising the distribution of food – and he came in only very occasionally – the cook would give me an extra half-pint of soup at the first serving.

With the exception of one or two ardent young members of the Party, the guards were mostly old campaigners, the majority having seen service in the 1914–18 war. They were tired of the war, and even as early as 1942 were quite convinced that the Allies would win. One of the sergeants spoke some English, and when he was in charge, he would spend hours talking to me.

The treatment of the prisoners was no more brutal, I suppose, than in our own 'glasshouses'; but it was certainly harsh and often horrifying. Everything had to be done at the double, though I successfully resisted this, maintaining that it was inconsistent with my dignity as an officer.

After the first morning, which was freezing cold – there were several feet of snow outside – I had no complaint of my own treatment. On that morning, however, I was taken into the prison yard for solitary exercise by two young guards who were little more than boys. The sudden fresh air and the intense cold made me dizzy, and though I tried to explain to them and staggered about quite genuinely, they made me run backwards and forwards the length of the yard. Every time I passed them they hit me across the knee with a rifle-butt. I fell several times and they kicked me in the ribs until I got up. Eventually I fainted and, when I came to, the prison doctor was bending over me massaging my heart.

At half-past four I was fetched by one of the Luftwaffe corporals who had met me at the airport, and taken to a large building at the corner of Wallstrasse, which I subsequently discovered was the Luftwaffe General H.Q. For half an hour I waited with my guard in a splendid anteroom, sitting on an elegant chair, and studying fine paintings on the walls by leading Latvian artists, whose work I had known before the war. Several Luftwaffe officers passed through the room regarding us with open curiosity. I was still bearded, stinking and tattered, and must have presented an extraordinary appearance.

Presently a Luftwaffe colonel, resplendent in grey breeches with a scarlet band down the outer seams, highly-polished boots, and the insignia of the Knight's Cross of the Iron Cross at his throat, came through, smiling graciously in our direction. Five minutes later an equally splendid Luftwaffe major beckoned us through into a dazzling apartment.

Seated behind a desk was a stout man wearing a goatee beard. I had heard much about Goering's self-designed white uniform for his Luftwaffe, and now I saw it for the first time – a stylishly-cut, double-breasted, wide-lapelled white jacket with gilt buttons and gold braid on the shoulders, the whole effect set off by the Knight's Cross of the Iron Cross with oak leaves and diamonds.

'The General asks you to be seated,' said the interpreter.

The simple sentence was a timely warning that once again I must be on my guard, for I had begun to sit when I had heard the General say, '*Bitte, Platz nehmen, Herr Hauptmann.*'

For a quarter of an hour the General fired questions at me. They were of wide application and quite unconnected with my self, about the position at home, public opinion there and so on. When he dismissed me, I apologised for my uncouth appearance and my smell.

'Perhaps you would like to be shaved?' he asked.

'Very much,' I replied through the interpreter.

'The Captain is to be shaved,' said the General to the colonel, who was his Chief of Staff.

'The Captain,' said the colonel to my escort, 'is to be shaved.'

After breakfast the next morning I was taken to the barber's shop and given a shave and a haircut. At ten o'clock I was escorted once more to Headquarters, where I was received by the Chief of Staff in his office. A major and a captain were sitting at opposite ends of a settee.

The Colonel had before him an abbreviated version of my statement to Nädlinger, which he consulted while asking me a few innocuous questions. This done, he carefully and shrewdly probed me to find out my opinion of the Russians and to test my knowledge of European political affairs. Although the interpreter was present, we spoke French.

At the end of the interview he asked if I had any complaints about my treatment in prison. I told him of the way I had been exercised the previous morning, that I could not sleep because of the hardness of the boards, and that I should be grateful for a bath.

When he finally dismissed me, he said to my escort:

'The Captain is staying here for some days. The General has ordered that he is to receive every respect due to his rank as an officer. He is to be shaved daily. He must be allowed to bathe and is to be given clean underclothes. He will receive an officer's ration of food and tobacco. If there are books he can read, he may have them. These orders will be sent to the prison in writing, but you are to tell the Commandant of the General's commands, which are to be put into effect at once.'

During the afternoon the sergeant on duty, a pleasant young man in the Artillery, came to me. He apologised for the fact that there would not be a better cell vacant until next day, gave me soap and a towel and took me to the shower. He stayed with me, telling me not to hurry and chatting in so friendly a fashion that in order not to appear boorish I had to answer him, which I did with a good deal of stammering, searching for words and making grammatical mistakes to keep up the pretence of my not knowing German.

When I got back to my cell a soft, thick straw palliasse and two blankets were on the bed; and a few minutes later the sergeant came in with a couple of ounces of tobacco and a packet of cigarette papers. Whenever I wanted a light I must knock for the warder; matches were very scarce. He also brought a book showing the history of National Socialism in pictures, and apologised for the fact that all the books in the library were in German.

All these attentions, which changed my life completely, lifting it from squalor to decency, were too much for me. After the sergeant's departure I sat on the bed and wept. I strove hard to restore my equilibrium by assuring myself that there must be some motive behind it all.

It was New Year's Eve, and the staff were having a noisy party which went on into the early hours of the morning. Just after midnight the sergeant came to my cell with a piece of cake and a mug of hot coffee, which was sweetened but without milk, and wished me a happy New Year. I do not think it was thoughtlessness on his part, but simply that he did not know I was under sentence of death. My morale, however, had so much improved since the afternoon that the irony of his wishes amused me, and he looked at me in amazement when I went off in fits of laughter.

Having discovered that I would not be returning to Tallinn for a time, and that here in Riga there were levels of authority I had never hoped to contact, I decided to produce my scrap of paper. The English-speaking sergeant was on forty-eight hours' leave, and it was January 3rd before I saw him again. This was the first time I had seen him since my change of status, and he was quite willing to co-operate when I told him that I had a very important communication to make to the Chief of Staff. After I had given him brief details, he immediately brought me paper and pen, and I wrote a letter to the colonel in the following terms:

Sir,
I have the honour to submit to you the accompanying piece of paper and explanation.

    As I was about to enter the aircraft which flew me on my operation, Captain Lovat handed me a letter from Major Beech containing good wishes and the following final instructions:—

On and after April 10, 1943, you are to listen on your 'A' frequency at 17.00 hrs. G.M.T. and 23.00 hrs. G.M.T. daily. You are to listen, but you are not to reply under any circumstances. This is most important.

Please initial this letter when you have read it, and return it to Captain Lovat.

I was so excited by my impending departure that I felt it would be wiser to make a note of these instructions and the only paper I had was a piece such as we now use in England for making our own cigarettes. This piece of paper is attached to this letter.

I screwed the scrap of paper up into a ball, and pushed it down the corner of one of my pockets. It has been overlooked in subsequent searches of my clothes, and I had completely forgotten the incident until I found the paper on December 24th. I told the sergeant about it on our way here, and he told me to keep it until I returned to Tallinn. For this reason I have not handed it to you before. I regret that I have not remembered it until now, as I believe it to be of some significance.

Further, I should like to offer my services in any capacity for which the authorities might think me fit, to work against the Jews and Bolsheviks. You already know my views on this point.

I respectfully suggest that in view of my wide experience of propaganda and broadcasting, gained while I was with the B.B.C., I could best be used broadcasting to England.

I have the honour to be, Sir,

Your obedient servant,

RONALD SETH,

Flight-Lieutenant, Royal Air Force

The sergeant, having read this through, promised to send it to Headquarters by runner at the earliest opportunity on Monday morning.

At ten o'clock on Monday I was taken once more to see the Colonel, who was alone in his office. He sent away both the interpreter and escort, and then pulling up a chair, offered me a cigarette and said in French:

'Captain Seth, since you have been here the Commander in Tallinn has sent me four or five telegrams – you can see them here – demanding your immediate return, so that your execution may be carried out without further delay. This morning I have sent the Commander a telegram in which I have said that the General and I, as well as our advisers here, believe that a living Captain Seth will be of much more use to Germany than a dead one.

'You are an intelligent and educated man, and you will understand better than most ordinary men in the West how things are with regard to the Jews and Bolsheviks. Perhaps you do not believe in providence, but I do; and I firmly believe that you have been sent to us by a Divine Power to undertake a mission on our behalf. What that mission will be, I do not know; but in time it will be revealed to us.

'We hoped that you would be here before Christmas, but apparently our signals were unavoidably delayed. That they arrived after providence had intervened on your behalf further convinces me that you have been especially chosen. We hope that you will quickly forget your gruesome experiences in Tallinn.

'We intend to send you as soon as possible to the Air Ministry in Berlin, where we hope that friends of ours will find you something useful to do. We know that we can rely on an English gentleman, who is also an officer in the Royal Air Force, not to betray our trust.'

During this speech my feelings almost overcame me. This was reprieve! I was not going to die – at least, not yet – and what I had long been hoping for had fallen right into my hands. It would be difficult and I should have to be clever. I felt faint with excitement, and it must have shown in my face for the Colonel went to a cabinet and poured me out a glass of sherry.

'Drink this, Captain,' he said. 'There is such a thing as an Omnipotent Being. You are a fortunate man, for you have had a revelation of His workings.'

At that moment there was a knock on the door. The Colonel opened it and a murmered conversation went on in the office beyond. When the Colonel returned he had a paper in his hand, which he read in silence as he sat at his desk. Then he looked up, carefully removed a long ash from his cigar, and said:

'You have written me a letter. What do you think this message means?'

Here was the critical moment which I had so often rehearsed to myself. I answered as firmly as I could:

'You know, sir, that my instructions included organising sabotage groups along the railway from Tallinn to Leningrad. I believe that this message may refer to a proposed counterattack by the Russians, timed to begin some time after April 10th, and that I was to have held myself in readiness to carry out the sabotage on receiving special orders.'

He considered this explanation for a moment.

'Yes, you may be right. I must take this to the General at once. It is very important,' he said. He got up, and I stood before him. 'We shall send you to Berlin as soon as it can be arranged. It may take some days, but do not think you are forgotten. While you are waiting I want you to consider every possible way in which you can help us. Let me have daily in writing whatever you may think of. I will give orders that you are to be well supplied with paper and ink. If you are in need of anything else, ask the Commandant for it.' He shook my hand. 'Goodbye, and good luck, Captain,' he concluded, smiling.

The sergeant did not share my elation when I told him what had happened. He reminded me that I should not think that my execution was cancelled, merely that it was postponed and could be put into effect at any time. But I refused to let my spirits he damped and told myself that he was a lugubrious fellow.

For the next ten days I wrestled with my impatience. I was subdued enough to recognise the danger of my position. Any outsider would immediately label me 'traitor'; and yet, when I thought it over, it would be worth while becoming an object of scorn and hatred if only I could get to a microphone or in some way communicate with home. To achieve this I was quite willing to perjure my soul.

Most of the day I worked out my ideas for radio and other forms of propaganda, and each day my ideas were forwarded to the Chief of Staff. In one of my letters I wrote:

It has always surprised the British authorities that the German authorities have not made greater use of pamphlets dropped by aircraft; I suggest that a series of pamphlets called AIR MAIL should be prepared and dropped at regular intervals over England. These pamphlets should take the form of letters from a prisoner of war to his wife on the lines of the three examples attached to this letter.

I prepared three examples incorporating in each of them the coded information that I wished to send home. I knew that if these letters were dropped, copies would sooner or later reach my superiors, who would recognise the messages.

The radio propaganda talks I prepared also in the form of letters, again working in messages. The days went by quickly, and as each batch of ideas was sent off I began to feel that 'Operation Blunderhead' might not, after all, be the fiasco that it had been up to now. My main concern was not to overdo my eagerness and thereby create suspicion.

During the afternoon of January 14th the Artillery sergeant burst in like a whirlwind to announce that I was leaving immediately for Frankfurt-am-Main. Numerous forms had to be filled in, as usual whenever I moved, and these had to be signed and countersigned before I could be handed over to the two Luftwaffe guards who were to be my escort.

We left the prison and walked to Luftwaffe Headquarters to pick up packs, rations and my dossier. It was extremely

133

cold and the sky was overcast. At the moment, however, my spirits were rapidly rising at the thought that at last I was on my way and that the success of my plans might soon be achieved. My escorts were an interesting and ill-assorted pair. One was a tall, thin, bespectacled man of about thirty, slow in movement and decision. The other was short and dark, with a glowing complexion and a bubbling sense of humour. He was a regular in the Luftwaffe, and the other's indecision irritated him intensely.

The station was crowded with soldiers from the Finnish, Leningrad and Latvian fronts going home on leave. When we got there at half-past four, the train — due to leave at five o'clock — was already drawn up at the platform, but was so crowded that there was no room for us. Instructions had apparently been given that my two escorts and I were to travel in a compartment by ourselves. The one in charge began to wave papers, and to some effect, for at the end of an hour another carriage was shunted on to the train.

It was a third class carriage with hard wooden seats, but it should take only a few hours at most to reach the Lithuanian-Prussian border. The greatest drawback was the lack of lighting and heating. We were told, in answer to enquiries, that we could not have lights because there was no blackout, but that as soon as the carriage had been coupled to the train, there would be some heating. We were shivering when, with Latvian punctuality, the train steamed out at seven o'clock, two hours late; as yet there was no sign of any heating.

After the worst train journey of my experience, we arrived at Tauenroggen, on the Lithuanian side of the border, thirteen hours later. Here the train was emptied and both officers and men were directed to the delousing station. Before being allowed into Germany every man had to get a certificate of non-infection.

This station was my first experience of German military organisation at its best. Just over two thousand of us disembarked from the train at eight o'clock. The last man passed from the delousing quarters to the canteen at a quarter to ten. Here we were served free of charge with bowls of hot soup and coffee. Later we were provided with rations for two days, consisting of a pound of black bread, an ounce of fat, two ounces of sausage, and twenty cigarettes.

At four o'clock in the afternoon the two thousand were drawn up in parties for re-embarkation. When our leader produced his papers, we were permitted to go on ahead to the train, on which a third class compartment had been reserved for us.

Punctually at four-thirty it pulled out as scheduled, and at eight o'clock we arrived in Berlin, having made a wide detour through East Prussia. The famous St Tomas Keller, which in peace-time was a fashionable rendezvous, had been converted into a hostel for troops in transit who had to wait for connections. After a wash and shave, we had a free lunch, then at five o'clock we got into the train for Frankfurt. Once more a compartment had been reserved for us, but this time, as the train was crowded with soldiers and favoured civilians who had been fortunate in getting travel passes, we allowed those who wanted to do so to come in.

The heat was very oppressive. I was still physically in pretty bad shape and the discomfort made me feel tired and faint, so I was very glad when we arrived at Frankfurt. I now learnt that my ultimate destination was the R.A.F. Reception and Transit Camp, Durchgangslager West, known as Dulag West, at Oberursel, about fifteen miles north-west of Frankfurt. This meant our taking a suburban train to the Frankfurt Central Station, from which the trains ran to Oberursel. As the first train did not leave until six o'clock, we spent three hours in the station waiting-room.

At a quarter to seven we reached Oberursel. It was still dark, and the tram to the Dulag, which was some way out of the town, was not due to start for more than an hour. It was very cold and thick snow covered the ground, so we got permission to wait in the station office.

When we alighted from the tram, a sergeant from the camp was waiting for us. Leading us by a short cut through a small plantation, he brought us to a group of one-storied wooden huts surrounded by a barbed-wire barricade. As we passed through the gates a sense of acute depression began to settle on my mind.

Although my stay in the prison at Riga had begun to dispel the hunger-pangs which I had suffered at Tallinn, I was still very weak. We had been travelling for sixty-one hours; I had slept only fitfully and was now so weary that when I came to be searched I took off all my clothes, hardly realising what was going on till I found myself standing naked in a cold room.

I don't know how long I stood like this, but it seemed a long time before I was given back my shirt, underpants, pullover and stockings, and a pair of khaki knee breeches. My leather jacket, storm-jacket and boots were to be kept for a more thorough search. It was only when I heard this that I remembered that the packet of letters I had written to my wife was still in the pocket of my storm-jacket.

CHAPTER 8

LUFTWAFFE INTELLIGENCE

WHEN a fighting man is made prisoner in war time he is taken first to a reception and transit camp where he spends several days in solitary confinement, except when being interrogated by intelligence experts. Usually after three or four days he is transferred to a Stalag, if he is an N.C.O. or lower rank, or to an Oflag if he is an officer. Under the Geneva Convention no prisoner of war may be compelled to give any information other than his name, rank and number, and the name and address of his next-of-kin. At Dulag West, however, things were very different.

The camp, which was exclusively for air-crews, consisted of long huts divided into single cells by walls of beaver board. It was the Headquarters of Luftwaffe Intelligence 'in the field'.

I was put in Cell 37, which contained a bed, a stool and a table. On the bed was a mattress filled with wood-shavings, a sheet, a pillow, a blanket and an eiderdown-case, after the custom of southern Germany, where a thick eiderdown in a white case serves as a top sheet and blanket combined. The window was of frosted glass, and although the upper part was originally made to open, it was now nailed up and would not budge. The cell was heated by a large electric radiator much too big for the room, which was regulated from outside the cell.

The washroom and lavatories were communal. One was allowed to wash twice a day, but not before eight o'clock in the morning. For the lesser calls of nature a glass chamber-pot was provided. Mine was cracked and leaked, and it took me three days to obtain a replacement.

On my first morning, not knowing that reveille was not until eight o'clock, and that one was not allowed to visit the lavatories before then, however urgent the call might be, I pulled a knob near the door, which released a wooden indicator outside in the corridor, and when the guard came I explained what I wanted by signs and exclamations in English. But the guard shut the door in my face, merely saying, 'Later.' A second and third attempt had the same results; it was then that I discovered the cracked glassware.

This incident introduced me to the moronic guards, who, if not actually mental defectives, must have been very near the border-line. Their vocabulary consisted of the one word – *später*, which means 'later'. No matter what one asked them, the answer was always the same, whether it made sense or not.

According to the Geneva Convention prisoners of war

must be provided with rations of the same standard as those allotted to the garrison of the detaining power. Towards the end of the war it was common knowledge that this provision was never honoured, the excuse of the German High Command being that there was a general shortage of food. From November, 1944 this was true, but I simply do not believe that at the beginning of 1943 the German garrison forces were on the low level of rations served at Dulag West.

The food and conditions were almost as bad as those in the Tallinn prison. Ordinary prisoners, it is true, were allowed cigarettes and books; but I was classified as a dangerous prisoner and was therefore forbidden to smoke or read.

Except for brief intervals for food, I slept soundly that night. Next morning my boots were returned to me, but when I asked for my other clothes I was told I would get them later. At about midday a blustering sergeant took me to an empty cell adjoining mine, and through the thin walls I could hear him ransacking my room. What he was searching for I do not know, but he seemed disappointed when he came back to fetch me; so I thought it a good opportunity to confess in my carefully broken German to the packet of letters in my storm-jacket.

'They've already been found,' he growled. 'And it's a bad look-out for you.'

At first I was worried, but when I thought it over I realised that the code would probably take years to break; in any case, I had done a good job on the letters, so that I would have to brazen it out and show that they were simply the innocent letters of a condemned man to his wife.

It was about three o'clock in the afternoon when Captain Fritz, of Luftwaffe Intelligence, came to see me. He offered me a cigarette and told me to sit down.

'Why on earth have you been sent here?' he asked. 'We can't understand it.'

'I've no idea,' I answered. 'The Chief of Staff in Riga told me I was being sent to Berlin to see if the Air Ministry could find me something useful to do there.'

'Why should you be found something to do?'

'Haven't my papers arrived?' I said.

'They have. But there are so many I haven't had time to study them. Perhaps you will tell me briefly about yourself?'

After I had told him what had happened up to my arrival at the camp, he made no comment, but got up and left me.

On Tuesday morning they began work on me in earnest. I was taken to a room where four or five officers were sitting. I noticed that each held a document, which I soon discovered to be a copy of my dossier. I was not allowed to sit, but was made to stand at attention. For several hours I had to stand like this without swaying or even moving from one foot to the other. At the slightest movement I was barked at and told to keep still.

The room was a surprise to me and an extremely disconcerting one, for on the walls were maps marked 'Convoy Rendezvous Points', 'R.A.F. Squadron Movements', 'Flak Concentrations', and so on. The secret information displayed on the walls was considerable, but throughout my interrogation, which lasted five days, I was continually surprised, for there seemed to be very little they did not know. At one point, for example, I was asked:

'How is it you are designated as belonging to the Special Duties Branch?'

'How do you know that?' I said.

'You will answer the questions, please. But since you ask, you will no doubt recognise this.'

The officer who was questioning me held out a copy of the Air Force List, which must have been dated between June, 1941 and September, 1942. During the war this List was treated like a secret document, being kept in the Adjutant's safe on all stations. Access to it was allowed only to officers, and in my experience only in the presence of the Adjutant.

My questioners' detailed knowledge of my career was more than intimidating. I had arrived at the O.T.U. at Pershore as an Acting Pilot-Officer under training in

Intelligence. Sharing my office was another Pilot-Officer named Francis, who was promoted Acting Flying-Officer, Assistant Operations Officer just before I left the O.T.U. One of the questions shot at me was:

'Was Flight-Lieutenant Francis the Regional Control Officer at Pershore while you were there?'

'No,' I answered; and another officer remarked, 'Pershore did not become a Regional Control station until after the prisoner had left.'

The interrogation was based on my Tallinn statement, but instead of going through it chronologically, they jumped about, and it was a tremenduous effort to answer correctly. I was at the disadvantage also of being questioned in English. When I had been questioned in German the time-lag caused by translating the questions gave me a chance to formulate my answers.

Not all the officers were there at every session. Sometimes I was harried alone by a fair young man who was an ardent Nazi and obviously out for my blood.

The same ground was covered in session after session, and if ever I made the slightest slip in dates – which I did deliberately from time to time, to cover up the fact that I had learned my lesson from Major Vogl's notes – they sprang on me like hawks. The lack of food rapidly began to undermine my resistance as well as my morale. One day the interrogators concentrated on my lack of papers, particularly of maps. (I was extremely glad I had got rid of mine in the Kiiu Aabla forest, for they would certainly have revealed my plan.)

'Do you really expect us to believe that the British Secret Service had no maps of the Port Kunda area? How did you expect to find your way about?'

'I know the country inside out. I lived there for four years. I knew the Port Kunda area by heart.'

The officer pounced on this triumphantly.

'Then draw us a map of the Port Kunda and Kohtla Järve area.'

He thrust a pencil and paper towards me and sat back, basking in the imminent admiration of his superior officers. But his triumph was short-lived, for at the end of ten minutes I presented the tribunal with a detailed map of the area, which was immediately compared with their own maps. I believe that if they could have permitted themselves to unbend, they would have congratulated me.

The officer nevertheless had the last word. That night, weak with hunger and fatigue, and not a little afraid, I went to sleep early. How long I slept I don't know, but I woke up bathed in sweat and breathing with difficulty. The temperature of my room was higher than that of a Turkish bath.

I got up and pulled the indicator knob; but no one came. I was panting heavily and my heart was pounding in my ears. I banged on the door and shouted, but the only answers I got were protests from the cells on either side. Soon my head began to swim and I sank down on to the floor. It was easier to breathe there, and I lay full length on the boards, fighting for breath. Presently I thought that if I broke one of the top windows I might get some relief: I should be disciplined, of course, but it would be worth it. I groped for my boot to use as a missile, when suddenly the light was switched on, the door was flung open, and the sergeant came in with two guards. One of them held me, while the other tore off my undervest and pants, in which I had been sleeping. Stark naked, I was dragged out to the compound. There was still snow on the ground and a sharp frost in the air, and the sweat pouring from my body seemed to freeze in a casing all over me. Soon I began to tremble all over, and not only my body but my mind as well became numb. After a while I was dragged indoors again.

But I was not taken back to the cell; I was taken to the office. There the questioning began again. I could only mumble incoherently, and the three officers who were interrogating me grew angry. But I could not take in their questions properly. My head swam and the skin of my skull felt as though it were stretched tight. Finally my incoherence made one of the officers so angry that he picked up a heavy paperweight from the desk and hurled it at me. It caught me between the legs and a blinding pain shot up through my belly. There was a short pause; then as the pain receded, they made one last effort.

'We have reason to believe that you contacted someone during the ten days before you were caught. If you do not answer, you may be shot. You realise that?'

'You may do what you like,' I shouted. 'I can't tell you what didn't happen.'

'You must answer our questions.'

I couldn't take it any longer, and I broke down in tears.

The next day they left me alone until the afternoon, when Captain Fritz came into my cell, accompanied by a sharp faced man in civilian clothes, with pig-like, piercing eyes and a shaven head.

'This gentleman is Assistant-Commissar Fischer, from the Gestapo,' said Fritz.

In spite of what I had already suffered at the hands of the Wehrmacht and the Luftwaffe, I had somehow imagined that it was preferable to be their prisoner than the Gestapo's. More than anything else I dreaded this, and I was afraid they would stop at nothing to get information from me which neither the Wehrmacht nor the Luftwaffe had so far succeeding in extorting.

'The Assistant-Commissar wishes you to tell him your story,' said Fritz.

The Assistant-Commissar did not speak English, so Fritz

translated for him. He asked me no questions, and when I had finished there was a pause before he answered in a thin, high-pitched voice.

'I don't believe you, my friend.'

That was all he said, and I knew that unless providence produced a miracle, these words were my death-warrant.

The next morning my interrogators made a final attempt to break me. But by now, convinced as I was that only death remained, my morale improved and my obstinacy was revived. Before they had got far I shouted, 'For God's sake, shoot me, but stop asking me questions I cannot answer!'

During the afternoon I was taken from my cell to a car, where Fischer and a typical Gestapo thug were waiting. My storm-jacket was now returned to me, having been searched so thoroughly that all the seams were slit and the kapok lining was coming out. They had not bothered to mend it, and my trousers too, were beyond repair; but a kindly old guard gave me a pair of R.A.F. trousers from the store. As I got into the car, he whispered in German, 'God watch over you, my boy.'

This unexpected kindness, the only sign of feeling that had been shown me since I had arrived, brought tears to my eyes again.

CHAPTER 9

ON REMAND

I<small>T</small> was about five when we arrived at the
Untersuchungsgefängnis – the Remand Prison – at Frankfurt.
The guards were inclined to be disgruntled and off-hand
until they recognised my escort, Assistant-Commissar
Fischer. Then their manner changed and they could not
perform his wishes quickly enough. This was particularly
true of the reception clerk, a little, bespectacled man with
a Hitler moustache, who increased his height visibly each
time he performed the Nazi salute.

I was suffering from a good deal of pain, caused by the
swelling of my testicles after the officer had thrown his
paperweight at me. The indifference to my fate which had
sustained me during the morning had dwindled as I sat
in the car regarding the back of Fischer's bullet head, and
had given place to a nervous reaction, in which fear for
the future predominated.

By the time we arrived at the reception office I was
pretty well all in, for the walk upstairs had been almost
too much for me; and when the little clerk suddenly
snapped: '*Sprechen Sie Deutsch?*' I replied too readily, '*Nein.
Ich habe kein Deutsch.*'

The little man pounced triumphantly, and looking towards Fischer for approbation, said: '*Kein Deutsch? Und was ist "nein", wenn nicht Deutsch?*'

Fischer grinned back, well pleased, and a shiver went down my spine.

Presently he departed, leaving instructions that the account for my stay was to be sent to the Gestapo until the Gestapo's own prison had a cell to receive me. The receptionist handed me a card on which he had written: 'Seth, Ronald, *Polizeihaft* [Police Arrest], 23.1.43,' and handed me over to a uniformed guard, who led me through heavy iron doors into the prison.

In the small office, in the presence of three prisoners who happened to be there, I was again stripped and searched, though this time it was little more than a formality. My injury caused a small stir, and I was asked through one of the prisoners, who spoke some English, if the Gestapo had already been at work on me. When I replied that Luftwaffe Intelligence was responsible, eyebrows were raised, and someone asked:

'Are you such a dangerous prisoner, then?'

'So dangerous,' I answered, 'that I am permanently under sentence of death.'

'Ah,' said the warder. 'You are not an ordinary soldier, then; you're a saboteur?'

Instinct warned me to deny this, because a saboteur

is rightly reviled by any man who is on the opposite side.

'No, not a saboteur,' I said, 'just an ordinary spy.'

There was a chorus of surprise, and one of the warders, who, it seemed to me, took a considerable risk, tried to comfort me.

'Ah, well, not all spies are shot.'

His view seemed to be shared by the others, for after a second's silence, one of the prisoners remarked by way of getting a laugh, 'No – some are hanged and some beheaded.'

On this cheerful note I was taken to Cell 45 on the ground floor. It was furnished with an iron bedstead, which folded up against the wall during the day, a small table, a stool, a commode and a cupboard, containing a few things for washing and for keeping the cell clean. A book of prison rules hung from a nail above the door.

The bed linen was changed once every three months; socks, shirt, handkerchief and tie once a week; and in winter we got clean underpants once every six weeks. The prison uniform consisted of blue denim jacket and trousers, a small round hat and wooden-soled pantouf-fles. As I was only a 'guest' in the prison, until the Gestapo could find room for me, I kept my own clothes, as did some of the more influential Germans on remand for civil, as distinct from political or felonious, crimes.

I had not been long in my cell before supper came round. Good-behaviour prisoners, known as *Hausarbeiters* or house-workers, did domestic chores about the prison, such as cooking, cleaning the corridors, sorting the linen, laundering and distributing the food. In return they received certain privileges, a little extra food, a cigarette now and again, and, perhaps the most valued of all, permission to talk and not to be shut up in their cell all day long. The *Hausarbeiters* were prisoners whose cases were not likely to be heard for several months.

Supper consisted of a small pat of Limburger cheese, a slice of black bread, and a bowl of rose-hip tea. Half an hour after supper, at about six o'clock, the lights were put out, and if one was not in bed by that time it was difficult to settle down comfortably for the night.

The more I thought about it, the more certain I became that I should never be able to resist any more torture. I was in an extremely nervous state, as a result of my treatment at Dulag West, and Fischer's cold words still rang in my head. For a long while, in growing mental anguish I tossed about on my bed. Finally, I got up from it and rolled up the black-out. Then with some difficulty I contrived to fix my leather belt, which the Norwegian airman had given me in Riga prison, to one of the window bars, leaving just enough at one end to make a noose for my neck. I was standing up on the stool to do this when my legs began to tremble so violently that the stool clattered against the iron bedstead. In a moment the light was switched on, a key rattled in the lock, and the night-warder came in. He ordered me to get down, which I did, then I sat on the bed and wept. He came and sat beside me, and put his arm around my shoulders.

'Let me die,' I sobbed, 'I want to die. I can't stand it any longer. The Gestapo will torture me. I'm finished.'

He was a man of well over fifty, with the Iron Cross on his pocket and decorations from the 1914–18 war strung across his breast.

'I've been a soldier too, my son,' he said, 'and I have two boys, who are all I have, fighting in Russia. Being a good soldier means having courage. You are an Englishman as well as a soldier so no one can doubt your courage. Remember, nothing is ever as bad as it seems. How old are you?'

'Thirty-one.'

'Are you married?'

'Yes,' I said; 'and I have a son of seven and a daughter of five.'

'And yet you would be a coward?'

This was not fair. He was using weapons which are indefensible against any man in my position. The appeal to one's family instincts is never a fair weapon. I wanted to tell him so, yet I knew he was using the surest weapon of all.

'Look,' he went on, 'promise me one thing. If I report this, they'll put you in the *straf* cell on bread and water: you'll have boards to lie on and nothing else, no blankets, no soup, nothing. If I don't report it, will you promise me never to do this again, no matter how bad things may seem?'

Once again, from a man who had fought my father, came the hand of friendship. The older men understood the futility of fighting. Their judgment had been matured and mellowed by war. Caught up in the holocaust again, they went about teaching by example. This kindness was a more effective weapon against my moral weakness than any appeal to family feeling. It made me weep all the more, copious, self-pitying tears, which were mixed now with tears of anger that I should ever have been so weak.

'Well?' he asked.

'I promise,' I said.

He saw me into bed and tucked in the covers as though I were a child.

'I'll leave the light on,' he said as he went out. 'Things are never so bad in the light as they are in the dark.'

I saw him only twice again. He was promoted shortly afterwards and disappeared altogether.

I awoke next morning to the sound of whistles in the corridor outside. By this time, accustomed to prison routine, I got up and made up my bed as I had found it — the sheet stretched over the mattress, the uncovered blankets hidden out of sight between the bed and the wall, the covered blanket in a roll at one end of the upturned bed and the pillow at the other end. As I was doing this a warder looked in to tell me to wash, and as soon as the door was opened again, to place the commode, dirty-water can and the fresh-water jug outside. I was then to polish the floor and do the dusting.

Shortly before seven the door was opened once more and I took in the emptied commode, the dirty-water can and the refilled jug. At the same time I was given a metal knife. Knives were collected again after supper and if anyone's knife was ever missing the whole floor was thrown into an uproar. Every cell was searched from top to bottom until it was found. Sometimes the *Hausarbeiter* would have mislaid it himself; sometimes a cell had been overlooked; much less frequently a prisoner had somehow managed to keep the knife back, and was given forty-eight hours in the *straf* cell.

At 7.30 breakfast was handed out, consisting of a bowl of coffee, and two ounces of black bread, which, on Wednesdays, Fridays and Sundays was spread with jam.

During the morning I was taken to another office, stripped and weighed. I tipped the scales at eight stone five pounds. Since being weighed on December 21st I had lost another eight pounds. For the rest of the time I sat waiting, wondering when the Gestapo would begin.

In the afternoon I was given a book. I learned later that every prisoner was provided with a book for the weekend. The English section of the prison library consisted chiefly of works by the lesser Victorian novelists, a section of English literature in which I was not well read.

On Monday morning the *Arbeitsmeister*, the warder in charge of the work which the prisoners were given to while away the time, came to me. He asked a few questions, went away and returned shortly with a large packet of advertisements for Dr Scholl's Bath and Foot Salts. These I had to fold in a certain way and make them up into bundles of fifty. The folding made my thumbs ache and took the skin off my finger-tips. But I was glad of the work, for although it was simple it distracted my thoughts.

From quarter to eight until midday I folded and packed. Then came lunch – a measured litre of soup, except on Tuesdays, Fridays and Sundays, when we were given a pound of boiled potatoes with some vegetable sauce.

Afternoon work began at one o'clock and went on until a quarter to six. During the afternoon the water-jug was refilled by a *Hausarbeiter*, who also carried a tray from which one could get fresh supplies of toilet paper or a needle and thread for small repairs, or soap or cleaning powder, and occasionally one could borrow nail scissors.

At six o'clock we had supper. This usually consisted of a bowl of rose-hip tea, black bread, a little fat and about half an ounce of sausage. Occasionally we got some fish-paste or a few potatoes instead of the sausage, and sometimes a small pat of Limburger cheese. Thus, for fourteen months I tasted no milk, sugar, meat, butter, fresh vegetables, fruit or fish. The prisoner who was healthy and well-fed when he arrived might just sustain life on this diet. After Dulag West, however, I was physically a good deal below the standard I had reached when I left Tallinn prison. Now the pangs of hunger returned with increasing fierceness and food became the most important thing in life.

Every day we were allowed twenty minutes exercise. The prison was a seven-storey building divided into two wings, each built in the shape of a hollow square forming a yard. In the middle of this yard was a circular flower-bed where a few plants struggled pathetically for existence. The prisoners from each floor took turns in walking round the flower-bed in single file, seventy-two paces to each round. The cells overlooked this yard, but as the windows were seven feet from the floor one could see nothing except a small part of the upper storey of the opposite block. There was no clock, and for a man in solitary confinement I cannot imagine a worse privation than not to know the time. For myself I devised a method of calculating it by the length of the shadows on that part of the opposite building which I could see through the window. It was only effective on sunny days, of course, and needed daily adjustment of a few inches. I could not tell the hours, but I knew that when the shadow reached a certain point, lunch would come, or the afternoon water-can would be put out, or supper would arrive.

Like all German prisons, the Frankfurt Remand Prison was always full, and usually had about three hundred and sixty prisoners. About a third of them were young French forced labourers, who had either refused to work or had committed petty crimes; another third were political prisoners, some of whom had been awaiting trial for about eighteen months; and the rest were ordinary criminals.

Once a fortnight, on Fridays, we were given hot showers. The baths accommodated five at a time, and three hundred and fifty prisoners were bathed in four hours. The time allotted to each man under the comforting water was only three minutes, but the sense of cleanliness did much to keep up morale. It was only a sense of cleanliness, for the soap ration, when it was available, was about a quarter of an ounce a month for all purposes. Once a week a barber shaved us in our cells; he would also cut our hair once a month, if we made an application beforehand.

In general, if one behaved properly the warders were kind and pleasant in a brusque sort of way. They had mostly been in civil employment before the war; one had been a waiter, another a tailor, another employed by a firm in

Frankfurt. The youngest, I should think, was well over forty-five; most were over fifty, and one was sixty-nine. The regular warders, who were younger men, had all been conscripted into the fighting services. The only trouble I had was with a youngish officer who had been invalided out of the Army, and who did everything he could to make life unpleasant for the *verfluchten Engländer*.

There were some advantages in being a Gestapo prisoner. One was carefully treated in case one should complain. Both warders and prisoners showed great interest in me. They pronounced my name in the German way – Sett.

Outside the door of my cell were two cards. One bore the letters PH, standing for *Polizeihaft*, with a small capital E in one corner, which signified that I was *Evangelisch* or Protestant. The other card bore the word *Papierarbeit*, which indicated to the warder on duty the work I was supposed to be doing.

On alternate Sundays there were Evangelical or Roman Catholic services, at which attendance was voluntary. I did not go, for though they would have created a diversion, I dared not risk the discovery that I understood German. I was once visited by the Evangelical pastor, who asked many questions not connected with my state of Grace, and went away angry when I would not answer him.

CHAPTER 10

THE GESTAPO

THE quota of work set me by the *Arbeitsmeister* was five hundred bundles, or two thousand five hundred advertisements to be folded and packed each day. I never achieved this figure, on principle.

A week after I arrived, I was put into a slightly larger cell on the third floor. The change was welcome, for there was a new set of sounds to accustom myself to; and for one who never spoke more than five words a day, to deduce what was happening from the sounds that one heard was an important mental exercise.

I had just finished lunch and washed up my bowl and spoon, when a warder came to my cell and announced: '*Komm! Gestapo!*'

In the reception office a young Gestapo agent, who looked as though he were got up to play the part of a G-man, fastened a pair of handcuffs on my wrists. They were several sizes too small and crushed my wrists painfully. Brandishing a revolver, he followed me downstairs and out into a waiting motor-car. We drove through the town to the Gestapo headquarters for the district, which was a large house in one of the residential suburbs.

Here I was hustled through corridors and eventually taken into an ante-room where I waited for about an hour, still handcuffed. Of all my periods of waiting, in cells, in ante-rooms or even when I was below the gallows, I think this was the most disconcerting period of all. The Gestapo, according to all that we had been told at home, was a highly qualified intelligence staff, with its own technique of interrogation. Its members were hard-hard-headed, tough and, unlike Nädlinger, Vogl and the Chief of Staff in Riga, devoid of all sentiment. No consideration of feelings, no kinship of brothers-in-arms-though-enemies, no tradition of military courtesy would sway their opinions. It was their duty to have my head, and I knew that I must therefore be condemned, if not out of my own mouth or by the facts, then by false evidence. If I would not say, of my own accord, what they wanted me to say, they would torture me until I did.

Nevertheless, the old streak of obstinacy in my nature had gradually begun to reassert itself during my week of waiting. I believed my wits to be still fairly lively, and I was determined that although it was unlikely that I should emerge from the contest alive, I would have a good run for my money; and now that the moment had struck, I wanted to take the measure of my enemy as soon as possible.

At last I was summoned. A man of between thirty-five and forty was sitting at a large desk. He had a plump, pleasant, rosy-cheeked face, and his delicate, white hands were manicured. This was Criminal Commissar Bütt. By his side sat a girl secretary at a typing-table, and against the wall were sitting a stranger and Assistant-Commissar Fischer. A chair had been placed for me to the left of, and facing, the Commissar's desk, and next to it a seat for the interpreter, *S.S. Standartenführer* Walter Schmitt.

Schmitt, as I afterwards discovered, was in civilian life a manufacturer of jewellery at Pforzheim, a town famous for its fine work. He had business connections with London, and before the war used to spend six months there every year. At the beginning of the war he had been conscripted into the *Waffen S.S.*, and having been seriously wounded at Dunkirk, had been invalided out with the rank of colonel and relegated to the Gestapo. He was about thirty-five, spoke English fluently, and was eager to let me know that he understood the English mentality, thus hoping he would be able to help me a little.

Bütt motioned me to the chair, smiling until he saw the handcuffs. Then his face changed suddenly, and he said in a loud, peremptory voice: 'Take those handcuffs off the Captain, and never use them on him again!'

Before my escort could comply with the order, Fischer's shrill voice was raised in protest.

'The prisoner is too dangerous to transport without handcuffs. I gave the order, and I insist—'

Herr Bütt silenced him angrily. 'I countermand that order, Herr Fischer. The Captain is not an ordinary criminal. He is a cultured gentleman. As yet, there is no reason to subject him to this indignity.'

I was prepared for them to attempt first of all to gain my confidence and ingratiate themselves with me. This small clash, however, showed me two things which I believed I could turn to good account. First, Fischer had already condemned me, so that I must be particularly wary of any questions he asked me: second, a feud existed between Bütt and Fischer; and as Bütt was the senior, with whom rested the final decision, I should do well to get him on my side from the start.

I therefore asked Schmitt to tell Bütt that I appreciated his order very much, and to assure him that I would never attempt to cause trouble while being brought to and from the prison. I realised, of course, that I could not hope to escape by making a sudden dash for liberty in the middle of a crowded city.

With the exception of Fischer, the members of the tribunal took their cue from Bütt. It was obvious from the beginning that they wished to impress upon me that, contrary to general belief, the members of the Gestapo were humane, understanding, highly intelligent and cultured people, and were criminally maligned by Jewish propagandists. The desire to be convinced of this themselves was

shown when, at the end of my interrogation, Bütt questioned me closely about the English police and the C.I.D.,
and was childishly pleased when I remarked that one would
always recognise an English detective from his feet, clothes
and gait, but that it was quite impossible to pick out a
Gestapo agent. I was also able to turn this desire to good
use myself, by insisting throughout my interrogation that I
had believed the anti-Gestapo propaganda instilled into us
during our training at home.

The Commissar conducted the examination from the
same questionnaire that Nädlinger had used. He also
adopted the same procedure, putting the question to
Schmitt in German, which Schmitt would immediately
translate and I would answer in English. Then he would
translate my answer into German, the Commissar would
dictate the question and answer to the girl, and she
would take them both down on her typewriter. If Fischer
or any of the others wished to ask questions or make an
observation, they were allowed to do so. Often at important points all five would fire off questions at me in rapid
succession.

I had the same advantage here that I had had with
Nädlinger and Vogl, in 'not knowing German'. Long before
Schmitt had finished translating the question, I had had time
to think of my answer. I was also helped a great deal by
the observations which they all made, believing that I could

163

not understand what they said, for I was able to judge how far I could go and what the general reaction was to my answers.

After their first clash, it was soon apparent that the antagonism between Bütt and Fischer was fairly deep. It was fortunate for me that Fischer was against me. Had he been *for* me, the more influential Commissar would automatically have been against me. Spurred on by Schmitt, who, after the first two days, showed a genuine liking for me and went out of his way to assist me, Commissar Butt undoubtedly saved me later on from the firing squad; although encouraged by Schmitt, the basis of his actions and reactions undoubtedly rested on his dislike of Fischer.

There were moments when Fischer's shrewd questions had me floundering. The first time this happened I made some remark which caused him to lose his temper and let out a flood of personal abuse. Though I could not show that I had understood what he was saying, the attack seemed wholly unjust, and I turned towards Bütt with a helpless look, as though seeking his protection. At once he retrieved me from my difficulty. After this, whenever I wanted assistance I adopted the same technique. I think Schmitt understood what I was doing and seemed to draw private amusement from it; but Fischer and Bütt apparently never realised the way I was using them.

During the first afternoon of my interrogation I realised that the boasted skill and intelligence of the Gestapo were indeed myths. Admittedly they were far in advance of both the Wehrmacht's and the Luftwaffe's Intelligence; but being now convinced that my mental agility was unimpaired, I accepted this new challenge to my wits, and as the days went by I determined once more to fight for an opportunity to make contact with home. My opponents, after all, did not really know England and the English mentality as they prided themselves that they did; nor did they really understand human reactions whenever these became complex. I was amazed at some of the extraordinary things I got away with. This was true not only of the Wehrmacht, Luftwaffe and Gestapo, but also of members of the S.S., who were men of the highest intelligence. Others I know can produce similar evidence. The efficiency of the German security forces, and particularly of the much-vaunted Gestapo, was really a delusion. My main care was to guard against over-playing. I soon realised that their apparent kindness and understanding was part of a policy to throw me off my guard, and as long as I constantly reminded myself of this, and also assumed a certain gullibility, I found that I was able to hoodwink my opponents in turn.

So at the beginning of 1943 I began a fight which grew in intensity as the weeks passed. I could never relax for a single moment, and there were times when the strain made me wonder if the fight was really worth it. Nevertheless, I directed all my energies and skill to gaining the confidence of the Gestapo. I assumed an air of complete frankness at all my interrogations. Whenever I knew that my information could not be checked, I misled my questioners as much as I could by plausible statements. Whenever I knew checking was possible, or that they already had the information, I told the truth, accepting full responsibility for what was important from the security standpoint and what was not. If I decided that a point was not important, I gave full information. If it was important, I pleaded ignorance, which in every case was accepted. I also plugged my assumed anti-Jewish and anti-Bolshevik sentiments continually, and this was much more effective with the thorough-bred Nazi Gestapo than with the less doctrinaire Wehrmacht and Luftwaffe.

Every minute point which I had made in my Tallinn statement was sifted by Bütt and his assistants and every detail was checked. Again and again I told myself that of all that I had done since leaving England, the most intelligent act was the purloining of Vogl's notebook and the learning of my answers by heart. It was now three months since I had been interrogated by Nädlinger, and I could never have reproduced for Bütt all the delicate shades with which I had coloured my story if I had not memorised it like a piece of poetry.

Three weeks after my interrogation had finished, Schmitt visited me in prison.

'For three weeks,' he said, 'we have had four people working on your two statements, and they can find not even the smallest detail in one which does not exactly correspond with the other.'

'Since I have been telling the truth, it hardly surprises me', I said.

It will have been obvious that my statement to Nädlinger contained three weak points. The first was the story I had told of the Wing-Commander's threats to compel me to undertake the operation. The second was the description I had given of my twelve days of freedom. I had said that I had been so frightened by anti-Gestapo propaganda that I dared not surrender, though I had set out fully intending to do so. I stuck to this point, however, for I now had my experience of torture in Tallinn and at Dulag West to support me. (Bütt insisted that the Tallinn men were not German Gestapo agents, but co-opted members of the former Estonian secret police.) The third weak point was my lack of maps and papers, though this had been partly settled by the map I had drawn at Dulag West. The Luftwaffe Intelligence had certainly, if unwittingly, helped me by reporting that they were completely mystified as to why a man so lacking in courage as myself had been sent on such a mission.

167

Point one certainly needed modification and expansion in order to reach the standard of accuracy required by the Gestapo, since they were proving much more difficult to convince than Nädlinger had been. We were approaching the end of the second session on Saturday morning when we came to this point. Schmitt had already told me that there would be no afternoon session, as January 30th was the Party's anniversary and was therefore a half-holiday. Sensing, for the first time, a distinct feeling of scepticism I said:

'All that I told the Wehrmacht was true, but I did not tell them the whole story. I had done something dishonest, something which I knew soldiers, with their high military conception of honour, would not understamd. I would like to tell you the whole story now, but it is rather involved and I want to get it right. Do you think the Commissar will give me permission to write it out over the week-end?'

I wanted desperately to have time to think this thing out. Fortunately Fischer was the first to see through my move and began to protest volubly. But Bütt silenced him, and after asking me one or two questions, gave me permission. On Sunday, therefore, I wrote out the following statement, as I remember it:

When I took my family from Tallinn at the beginning of the war, I had to leave behind all my money and we arrived in England without a penny. Owing to heavy business losses as the result of the war, my father was unable to help me, and to support my family I had to borrow money.

When I joined the staff of the B.B.C., my salary was only seven pounds a week, and with the high cost of living, having to rent a furnished house, and at the same time having to repay our friends, we were unable to make ends meet. [So far, this is the truth; what followed was fantasy.] We, therefore, began to get into debt with the tradespeople. As you will appreciate, with your knowledge of human affairs, as soon as a man gets into debt, the debt grows with the rapidity of a snowball. New debts are incurred in trying to pay off the old.

The house in which we were living was bombed, and we lost all our personal belongings. This added to our debts. Our second house was partially destroyed by a fire-bomb, and in order to cover our debts I had to borrow £80 from a friend.

We were then evacuated to the country, my uncle lending us the furniture for another flat. The friend who had lent me £80 then got into financial difficulties himself and pressed for the repayment of the debt. Not knowing where to turn, I pledged my uncle's furniture to a Jewish moneylender. I was then conscripted, and became unable to pay the interest on the loan when it fell due. The Jew immediately demanded the return of the capital, plus interest, and refused any other terms. He began at first to press and then to threaten me, and in order to gain time – though I did not know where I should get the money – I sent the Jew an unbacked cheque.

The cheque, of course, was returned by the bank, so through me my family was consequently threatened with disgrace. The Jew then announced that he would send the cheque to the Air Ministry.

I heard no more about it until the day I was summoned to the Air Ministry by the Wing-Commander. He then told me that if I did not accept the proposition that had been put to me I should be dismissed from the Service and handed over to the civil authorities, by whom I should undoubtedly be sent to prison. If, on the other hand, I accepted the proposal, all my debts would be paid and nothing more would be said. To save my family from disgrace, I accepted. Although I have always hated Jews on principle, this episode gives me a very personal grudge against them.

On Monday I took this statement with me to the Lindenstrasse and Schmitt translated it. There was silence until Schmitt came to the point about the dishonoured cheque. Bütt declared that the Air Ministry would never have taken such measures. Walter explained, however, that English law treats a dishonoured cheque much more severely than the German law, which merely imposes a fine. This satisfied Bütt, and the statement was put into the record.

When we came to point three, in spite of the map I had drawn at Dulag West, Fischer refused to believe that I had landed in Estonia without maps or documents. An acrimonious scene followed, which to me, as an onlooker, was not lacking in humour. Once again, Bütt overruled Fischer and accepted my word.

My interrogation was concluded on February 8th, having lasted between seventy and eighty hours. When I had signed the record, Bütt said that he would do all that he could to help me. Under the law I was, of course, still under sentence of death, which might be carried out at any moment. The papers would have to be sent to Berlin, and it would take several weeks before a reply could be received. He suggested, therefore, that I should go back to prison and try to forget the matter for the time being. Both he and Schmitt believed my story, and they at least would leave nothing undone to save my life. If there should be anything I had overlooked and might wish to tell them, I had only to send him a note asking for someone to visit me. I was not to write anything and give it to the prison authorities, by whom it would doubt-less be read, since the fewer people who knew anything about me, the better.

CHAPTER 11

SOLITARY CONFINEMENT

I RETURNED to the Remand Prison to begin another long period of waiting, a period which was physically more disastrous than any I had yet undergone.

I was still folding Dr Scholl's advertisements, and was growing heartily sick of the job. The action of folding was developing the muscles of my thumbs and forefingers to such an extent that I was now able to tear a packet of fifty advertisements in half. One morning the *Aufseher*, noticing the bulges in my hands, immediately decided to change my work. So I said farewell to Dr Scholl, having folded no less than fifty-seven thousand of his advertisements. My new work was making paper bags. My day's output was set at four hundred, but again I successfully resisted all attempts to get this quota out of me.

Nearly a month passed before I received my first visit from Schmitt, who told me he had been taken from his ordinary work by the *Kriminalrat* (a higher rank than Commissar) in order to prepare my case for presentation in Berlin.

'But isn't there something more you can tell us?' he asked, 'something which would absolutely convince the authorities in Berlin, who, after all, don't know you as we do. The Commissar thinks highly of your intelligence and courage and sincerity, and he believes that if we could get permission, we could use you best by sending you back to England.'

So here it was again! Even if the offer was no more than a bait to get more information out of me, it gave me hope once more – and a new idea. I decided at once to sow the seeds of a plan to get myself returned to England as a Nazi agent.

In order not to appear too eager, I protested to Schmitt that I had honestly told the Gestapo all I knew. But as Schmitt expanded his ideas, I let myself be persuaded little by little that I might be able to produce something suitable.

'I won't tell you anything that might involve harm for any of my countrymen,' I said, 'but if you will leave me some writing paper, I will see what I can do over the week-end.'

So the next afternoon I began to write, or rather to 'compose', for what I concocted would never have deceived anyone who knew England and the English really well. I decided that the golden rule must be *don't overdo it*.

The first of my essays concerned Mr Churchill. I had never seen him in my life, and all I knew of him was the sort of gossip-glorification with which most national heroes are surrounded. However, I tried to make out that I knew a good deal more about him.

The second and third essays gave false information on relatively unimportant subjects. The fourth, which I reproduce as well as I can remember it, was the one that helped me most.

The Republican League

My family is a very old one. We have been hereditary pages to the Kings of England for more than three hundred years. This has brought me into close contact with the Royal family, and my wife and I frequently dine privately at Buckingham Palace.

I have known the Duke of Windsor intimately for many years, from the time when he used to come to hunt at my aunt's place in Lincolnshire. As a result of a hunting accident in which he was injured a very close friendship sprang up between us, which has lasted to the present day. I last dined with him in October, 1936, shortly before he abdicated. He told me then that he was being forced into a position from which abdication seemed the only solution. He was very popular with the working people of England, and I am quite certain that there would never have been war with Germany had he remained King.

One Sunday I was at the Officers' Sunday Club, which was run by the Dowager Marchioness of Townshend at the Dorchester Hotel. In the bar I was overheard to express the view that England would never be able to withstand the ravages of war unless a republic was inaugurated under the presidency of a certain famous man. A little later I was approached by a very well-known K.C. [whom I named, as I took care to name everyone that I mentioned] who asked me to dine with him at his chambers in Gray's Inn the following week. I did not think this strange, as many kind people entertained Service officers who were alone in London.

When I arrived for the dinner, I was surprised to find that the only other guest was a high-ranking naval officer. After dinner our host brought the conversation round to my remarks about the possibility of England becoming a republic. After more close questioning, he said, 'Since I overheard your remarks on Sunday, we have been making close enquiries about you, and now wish to put a proposition to you. Before we do so, however, are you prepared to take a solemn oath that, whichever way you feel, you will not divulge to anyone what we shall tell you?'

To this I agreed, and he then went on to describe

a secret society called the Republican League, whose aim it was to effect a *coup d'état*, force the King to abdicate, and replace the present constitution by a republic, one of whose first aims would be to negotiate a peace with Germany.

'We are not a very large movement at the moment, but we are growing' [here I put in a string of names of influential persons said to be interested in the League] 'and are looking out for young men like yourself, who could talk to officers in your mess and recommend likely men to us for membership.' Would I do this? my host asked.

I said I would; but I have not given this information to the German authorities before because many of my closest friends are members, and if the vaguest hint of this got out, they would all lose their lives. I know that the League is short of funds. Perhaps, if I am returned to England, Germany would be willing to give them the help they need. But I do respectfully request that this shall be treated most secretly.

Needless to say, the whole account was a complete fabrication, and I offer the famous men I named a sincere apology.

I gave what I had written to Schmitt when he called at the prison on the following Monday. He was in a hurry, however, and was unable to go through it with me, but returned a week later to say that he had been able to make very good use of the information, especially that about the Republican League, which had been received with great interest.

A long time went by without my hearing another word. There were moments when my spirits were so low that I believed Bütt and Schmitt had been deceiving me, that there would never be any possibility of my achieving the goal I had set myself, and that my end must inevitably come soon. On one occasion I wrote to Bütt, offering my services in a labour battalion on the Russian front, hoping that if I could get there I might have a chance of escaping to the Russians. Often I was tempted to break my promise to the night warder and hang myself.

Towards the end of May, nearly sixteen weeks after the end of my interrogation, Schmitt suddenly turned up again. But only to say that no reply had yet come from Berlin. All he could do was to encourage me. It was small consolation, but it helped.

On June 5th, my birthday, I had one of the pleasantest birthday presents I have ever had – a glimpse of the sun, the first since October, 1942, almost eight months before. I could see the sunshine from my window of course, but never the sun. On this morning we were later than usual in going out for exercise, and on the last round I caught a fleeting glimpse of it over the edge of the roof. It was a sight that I shall never forget.

At the end of June I again wrote to Bütt, pleading to be given some information. On the previous day one of the prisoners had gone mad – the second since my arrival in January – and had been put in the padded cell, where he had howled and screamed incessantly until they took him away twenty-four hours later. My health now began to be seriously affected. Running sores appeared between my toes, and my feet started to swell. The pain was considerable, and the doctor either could not or would not, give me any relief.

Towards the middle of the month the warder, a man named Heilmann, who had only become a warder since the war, brought a prisoner into my cell to carry out some minor repairs. Contrary to regulations, Heilmann began talking to me. He told me about the German defeat in North Africa six months earlier, and said that the Allies had landed in Italy and were now marching on Rome. This was the first news I had had of the progress of the war since my capture.

As the days passed, my toes got worse, and often I was unable to get my boots on, so that I was unable to exercise. I think that at this time I was often over the edge of insanity; sometimes I would suddenly come to and find that I had done hardly any work. I seldom managed to make more than two hundred bags a day; often it was fewer, but the *Arbeitsmeister*, realising how ill I was, did not trouble me.

I do not know whether it was at the end of July or the beginning of August that I was taken from my cell and led into an empty room with a long table at one end, above which hung an immense Nazi emblem. Behind the table were five chairs and to the left a small table and a chair.

We had not been long in the room when a man came in through a door behind the table. He ordered the guards to wait in the corridor outside, and locked the door after them. Coming back, he spoke to me in English, telling me to sit down at the small table on the right. In spite of the pain and my confused state, I realised that here was Nemesis at last. They were even going through the farce of a trial.

Presently another man with a bulging despatch-case appeared and went to the table opposite. We were ordered to stand, as five men filed in silently and sat down at the long table.

I felt I must take some interest, so assuming perplexity, I asked the man sitting by me what it was all about; but he shook his head, indicating that I must be silent. A man sitting at the middle of the table then began to speak, but so rapidly that I did not catch what he said. Immediately the man at the small table opposite rose and read a short account of my landing on Kiiu Aabla, and then my statements to Nädlinger and Bütt. When he had finished, there was a whispered consultation between the five: then turning towards me, the man in the middle said:

'This tribunal of the People's Court finds you guilty of high treason against the Führer and people of the German Reich, and sentences you to death by beheading.'

It had all happened so quickly and my senses were so confused that I really did not know what to think or say. I found myself making a short speech, which was translated by the interpreter, in which I said that it would be foolish to kill me when, given the opportunity I could do useful work against the Russians and Jews. When I had finished, the court rose with no further word and filed out. As my 'prosecutor' closed the door behind him, the interpreter took me to the door, unlocked it, and handed me over to the warders, who took me back to my cell.

This experience practically finished me. Whether it was a trick or not, whenever I heard footsteps approaching, my heart seemed to stop until they passed by. Hourly I expected to be taken out and beheaded. Yet the days dragged on and nothing happened.

September came, and to add to my troubles, though my toes had partly recovered, the poison in them began to spread up my right leg, which became so swollen that I could only drag it along with great pain.

Then one day towards the end of the month, Schmitt suddenly appeared. He had a message from Bütt telling me not to worry, as Berlin had not yet given final consideration to my case. He seemed more shaken by my appearance than I was relieved by his. I really did not care to go on living, and death would have given me a refuge from my pain. Now his news brought a flicker of hope, but it did not last long.

By October my leg had swollen to almost twice its normal size, and a large lump had formed on my calf. The pain was excruciating, and the warder frequently came to warn me that unless I stopped my cries, they might think I was mad and take me away. I could move from one end of the cell to the other only by dragging myself along the floor. But when the doctor dressed my leg, he refused to let me stop working at my paper bags, and told the *Arbeitsmeister* that I was capable of producing the maximum.

'The infection is in his leg,' he said, 'not in his hands. He can still use them.'

Since my arrival in Frankfurt there had been many alerts, but the centre of the city had never been raided. Then one night at the beginning of October, shortly after lights-out, bombs began to fall. The prisoners started screaming and banging on the cell doors, but there was no sound of any warders. The sensation of being confined helplessly in a small space and unable to run for it, if necessary, was extremely unpleasant.

Eventually the warders unlocked the cells, and in the utmost confusion – all the lights had failed – the prisoners rushed to the cellars. I was able to move only with difficulty, and negotiating the iron staircase was so painful that every few steps I had to sit down. Presently I was all alone in the darkness, with bombs shaking the old edifice. At last I reached the ground floor, but I had no idea which way to turn. A red glow coming through the windows lit up the corridors. The connecting door between the wing I was in and the administrative offices was open, and I went through, occasionally calling out in English. But no one heard me, or if they did they took no notice. I could have laughed aloud. Here I was, the most dangerous prisoner in the *Untersuchungsgefängnis*, wandering about completely unguarded.

At the end of a passage on my right I saw a door standing open. I shuffled along to it, supporting myself by the wall, and pulling it open, found it led straight into the street.

Here was freedom – and I could not take advantage of it! With an hour or two's start, had I been all right, I might have got to the station and found a train for France.

As I was standing at the open door a bomb fell at the end of the street, and the blast sweeping up the narrow passage between the high buildings seemed to singe me as it went by. I moved inside and then heard footsteps not far away. A voice cried out:

'He! Wer ist da?'

'Sett. Ich verloren. Es ist nicht gesund heraus.'

It was a little warder, who in civilian life had been a waiter, and had shown me small kindnesses now and again. He wanted to know what I was doing, and when I told him, helped me down to the cellars where all the prisoners were herded together. There I fainted from the pain in my leg, and lay more or less unconscious until the 'all clear' went in the small hours.

The following days were chaotic. There was no light or heating and, worst of all, no water. For two days we were without soup, and were rationed to one tumbler of ersatz coffee. It was impossible to wash, and the commodes remained unemptied for six days. To add to my misery, the swelling in my calf burst, but the doctor refused to attend to me. His house had received a direct hit during the raid, his wife had been killed, and he had lost everything he possessed. With the bursting of the lump, however, the stiffness in my leg eased, the swelling receded and much of the pain went. For a time my morale also improved and my mind began to clear. Then, without any reason that I could discover, I was moved down to cell 75 on the second floor. It was so narrow that when I stood with arms outstretched I could easily touch both walls.

I had been unable to exercise for many days, but about the middle of October my foot and leg were so much easier that I decided to try to limp round the yard for a little while. As I was completing the first circuit and approaching the doorway, I saw coming into the yard a friend with whom I had done my wireless training. It was a considerable shock to me, as I have no doubt it must have been for him. With great self-control neither of us allowed any flicker of recognition to pass, in case it should be reported to the Gestapo.

Back in my cell, I began to be extremely apprehensive. I felt certain that this was a Gestapo trick, and decided that if possible I would get a note to my friend, warning him to say nothing that might give the game away. So after work that evening, I scratched a message on a piece of paper with a nail, and the following morning as I came in from exercise, I threw it through the open door of the cell which I calculated to be his from the place he occupied in the file as we walked around the yard. The warders, however, had been too wily. When I went to the showers at the end of the week I discovered that he was in a cell isolated from the rest.

My failure to get this note to him, and what we should say to avoid incriminating each other, should we ever be brought face to face, kept me on tenterhooks for days. It was a most uncomfortable feeling, for one wrong word from him might bring my whole story tumbling about my ears; and a misplaced remark from me might just as easily spell catastrophe for him.

But we never met, until one day in 1945, when we accidentally ran into each other in London. He had remained in the Frankfurt prison until after the invasion of France, when he was transferred to one at Torgau. Only by great persistence had he managed to extricate himself from it when the Americans and Russians joined up at Torgau in April 1945.

Towards the end of October, a Wehrmacht officer called Captain Gunther visited me and informed me that the Gestapo had handed me back to the Army. The Chief Military Prosecutor had decided that I was to be removed to Torgau and there court-martialled. Gunther, who had been appointed Prisoner's Friend, discussed my story with me for some time. When he rose to go, I asked what he thought my chances were.

'Very slight,' he said. 'Very slight indeed. The prosecution bears a grudge against you because of the message you gave to the General at Riga. It caused troops to be diverted just at the crucial time at Kharkov last March.'

This, then, was the last move. Neither Bütt nor Schmitt had been able to help me, and I knew the Wehrmacht would show me no quarter. It might save me a great deal of pain and trouble if I wrote a confession. I told Heilmann, the warder, who was to risk his life for me many times during the next few weeks, what I intended to do. But he stoutly refused to give me paper and pen.

'Much may happen between now and February,' he said. 'Don't give up hope.'

At the beginning of November I became very ill. Another large lump had appeared, this time on my right knee, and I could not move. My general condition was so low that I could not even dress myself, so Heilmann told me to stay in bed. As he saw me getting worse, at very great risk to himself he protested vehemently to the chief warder, whom he brought to see me. In my presence he told the great man that if he would not order the doctor to come, he himself would go to the Governor.

The doctor came, but he could do little for me, apart from bandaging my knee and giving me words of very cold comfort.

'They say you are to go to Torgau. You won't get there though: in six weeks this poison will have killed you. I have nothing which can help you.'

It was now that Heilmann showed himself to be entirely fearless. He smuggled apples to me, and insisted on my having his sandwiches, while he went hungry. The news, he told me, for he listened to the B.B.C. every night, was better and better.

There was one very excitable warder who had been seconded from a penal prison. He had a hustling manner which I thought at first was due to antagonism. After I took to my bed, he used to come blustering into my cell and in his fussy way try to cheer me. I began to dread his visits, for they broke the daze in which pain and weakness lapped me. One day early in November his intrusion was noisier than usual. Then I heard him saying, 'Get up! Get up! Dress quickly! 'stapo, 'stapo!'

'I can't dress,' I said. 'I can't walk.'

At this he became quiet and gentle, and helped me to get into my clothes. Then with my arm round his shoulder, and his own about my waist, he more or less carried me to the waiting room. There I found Schmitt.

'I have good news for you,' he said. 'We are taking you to Paris as soon as we can get your release, which I hope will be one day this week.' I tried to speak, but the words stuck in my throat. I felt his hand on my shoulder, and heard him saying:

'You must get better now. We have work for you to do.'

Already on the way back to my cell, strength seemed to come flowing back, and except for a hand under my elbow, I needed no assistance from the warder. I was still too weak to sit for long, however, so I made my bed and lay down on it. My mind was whirling. I could hardly realise that I really had achieved that for which I had been struggling so long. From now on my recovery was amazing. In three days, the lump on my knee burst and by the beginning of November I was strong enough to take exercise.

Early on the morning of November 14th, 1943, I left the Frankfurt *Untersuchungsgefängnis*, after 371 days of solitary confinement, and accompanied by Bütt and Schmitt, I boarded the train for Paris. In my pocket were forty-seven reichmarks and forty-seven pfennigs, which I had earned by folding 57,000 of Dr Scholl advertisements and making 67,000 paper bags.

CHAPTER 12

PARIS

SCHMITT and the Commissar were travelling light. They each had a rucksack containing a few personal necessities, and both had large empty suitcases, which Schmitt explained, were for 'presents. One can still get silk and food in Paris.'

While Bütt went to the restaurant car for lunch, Schmitt told me how he and the Commissar had tried to 'sell' me to their counter-intelligence in Paris. At first, the Paris authorities had agreed, but had afterwards changed their minds. Then the Chief Military Prosecutor had reclaimed me. But later on Captain Fritz, of Dulag West, had been posted to the Luftwaffe section of the *Geheimdienst* — the Secret Service — in Paris, where the second-in-command was a close friend of his. Bütt, on hearing this, had approached Fritz, who had managed, with Bütt's support, to persuade his chief to enrol me, though at the moment they had not decided what my work should be.

'If you play your cards well,' Schmitt said, 'you can do yourself, as well as us, a good turn. At least it will prolong your life; and the Commissar and I have fought for that as if our heads were at stake instead of yours.'

It was dark when we arrived in Paris, where Fritz's chief, Major Herr Baron Kliemann, was supposed to be meeting us. However, as there was no sign of him, Bütt went in search of him and returned a quarter of an hour later with a round-shouldered, bleary-eyed man whom he introduced as Dr Kilburg, Deputy Chief of the Luftwaffe Section of the Secret Service in Paris. It was not until much later, and then quite by accident, that I discovered Kilburg was Baron Kliemann, who took the most elaborate precautions to preserve his alias.

While we were waiting for Bütt to return, I asked Schmitt where I was to be accommodated. He said that he thought it might be in prison, though he and Bütt had argued against this. When we got into Kilburg's car he announced that he had booked rooms for us at the Hotel Monsigny, near the Opera. When we got there, Kilburg, speaking French, told me that until further notice I should be known as Georg Heydt, and warned me that I must never reveal my own name or even my nationality, since the French Resistance had their agents everywhere and would not hesitate to liquidate me if they thought I was working for the Germans.

The next day, when Schmitt returned from meeting Bütt and Dr Kilburg, he called me into his bedroom.

'For heaven's sake,' he warned me, 'don't tell anyone I've told you, but they are going to get you fit, then train you and send you back to England.'

He was moving about the room, changing his clothes as he said this, so luckily did not notice that the news, which was better than I could ever have hoped for, affected me so much that I couldn't answer him.

'You'll have to watch your step while you're here,' he said. 'Everything you do, every word you say, every thought that passes through your mind, will be reported. Go slow at first; do everything you can to get their confidence. And watch out for the Doctor. He's a Bavarian, high up in the Party. He's neurotic and quick-tempered and quite ruthless. They all think he's a bit mad, but he's certainly brilliant at his work. He has been made personally responsible for you, so get on the right side of him, and you'll be all right. If you upset him though, it'll be the end of you.'

It had been arranged that the Doctor should fetch me from the Monsigny before lunch on Wednesday and take me to my future billet. So after breakfast I said goodbye to Bütt and Schmitt, thanked them for all they had done for me, and once more perjured my soul by promising as an English gentleman not to betray their trust.

I had no food ration coupons, and as the Doctor did not arrive until three o'clock, I was extremely hungry and not in the best of tempers when at last he walked into my bedroom. But his apologies, in his curious German-French, were quite disarming. He addressed me always as 'Monsieur,' and treated me consistently with aristocratic courtesy and correctness.

We drove out to a villa in the suburbs, where a young man, who I subsequently discovered was half French and half German, lived with his French wife. This young man, whom I will call Hugo, was a highly expert amateur radio technician, and as a member of Kilburg's service his duties took him from time to time all over France to mend the transmitters and receivers of many German agents, whose sets were not to be entrusted to the French for repairs. His wife was called Yvette. Ten years older than himself, she had been married before at a very early age and had divorced her husband a few years later. She had once been beautiful but now had rather lost her looks.

The other members of the household were Bette, the old cook, Lucille, the maid, Gaston, her lover, who did odd jobs, chiefly going to the other side of Paris in search of food, and a dog called Grec. In the attics lived the owner of the villa and his wife, an old couple named Bertrand, who were both well over seventy. M. Bertrand, who was much travelled, knew England well and I do not believe that my assumed nationality ever deceived him.

To complete the family circle there was Yvette's sister, Mme Thérèse Lupin, who had a flat in Passy, and Hugo's sister, Simone, who lived in a house near the Jardins des Luxembourg. She had originally worked in Kilburg's office, but had given up the job to engage in more lucrative activities on the black market.

The house where I was to live was comfortable and well furnished. My room, which was on the first floor, was pleasant enough but it faced north and was rather cold. Round the house there was a large wild garden which had once been a place of beauty, and within five minutes' walk was the Bois de Boulogne.

When we arrived at the house on this first afternoon, Kilburg gave Mme Hugo and me very definite instructions. Until my German identity card was issued, I must not leave the grounds. If any callers came to the house, they were on no account to see me. I was to be given the best of food, and a liberal allowance would be made to Mme Hugo for my keep. He gave her some ration cards for me and then handed me 1000 francs for any odd things which I might need, promising that I would get a similar sum every week. Before he left, he said he would return in a few days.

Mme Hugo certainly fed me very well and tried to make me comfortable and happy. A small American radio had been put in my room, but as there was no aerial I could hear only the occupied French stations. From time to time Hugo brought me English books.

From the first moment I followed Schmitt's advice, and lost no opportunity of working my way into the

Hugos' confidence. It soon became evident that Kilburg had some sort of hold over both of them. I think I touched the fringe of this when I learnt later that before the war Mme Hugo was alleged to have been a Communist, and that her husband, having joined the French Air Force at the beginning of the war, had thus for a time been an enemy of the Germans.

Of the two, I believed I had more to fear from Mme Hugo than from her husband. He was a weak character, but kind-hearted, generous and tolerant. She, whose fear of Kilburg seemed to be the greater, was sycophantic towards him, and therefore a potential source of danger. Subsequent events proved that she was capable of inventing stories either to curry favour with Kilburg or to harm those she disliked. For the next eight months I therefore lived under an indescribable mental strain. I had to watch the inflexion of every word I said, every gesture I made, and even my facial expressions and the gleam in my eye. It was not easy to listen to, and sometimes participate in, constant attacks on the Allies. Night after night I had to smile and nod approval as the traitor, Jean Herold-Paquis, who has long since faced the firing-squad, concluded his broadcast commentary with, *L'Angleterre comme Cartage doit être détruite!* – 'England, like Carthage, must be destroyed!'

Gradually I built up my false background. Believing the Germans to be great snobs, I began to foster the idea of ancient connections, acquaintance with members of the Royal Family, intimate friendship with the Duke of Windsor (who was extremely popular in Germany both with the Party and others), my social hobnobbing with Mr Churchill and other leading British figures. All this, and the views I expressed from time to time were, I knew, faithfully reported to Kilburg by Mme Hugo, whom I regaled with fantasies for this purpose.

Within a short time the good food, the unlocked doors, the books and cigarettes, the fresh air and gentle exercise, the conversation and movement of people about me, made the prison pallor fade from my cheeks, put flesh on my bones and restored my health. In order to listen to the B.B.C. I rigged up an aerial, which I concealed in the shutter outside my window. It was a considerable risk, but the sound of the announcer's voice reading news which I knew I could believe, gave me a comfort which I would have risked much more to enjoy.

On the Saturday following my arrival Hugo took me shopping and fitted me out with clothes. It was not until the week before Christmas, however, that my identity card was issued. After further consideration of my cover story, Kilburg's department decided that it would be better if, with my fair colouring, I posed as a Scandinavian. Finnish nationality was chosen, as very few foreigners speak the language. So I became Sven Paasikivi, a nephew of the then Prime Minister of Finland (the present President of the Republic), by profession a diplomat, now resting in Paris after two years on the Russian front. To cover any English-French accent, it was explained that I had been educated in England and spoke English almost better than Finnish.

In spite of Kilburg's explicit instructions, I was introduced to Mme Lupin, Mme Hugo's sister. She was a constant visitor to the house, and it would have created an impossible situation if I had had to go into hiding every time she arrived. I was not averse to meeting anyone, for I believed I should still achieve something worth while, even if I could do no more than identify the collaborators that I met. Incidentally, my meeting Mme Lupin gave me a slight hold over her sister, for I was certain that if I ever threatened to tell Kilburg that she had introduced us, she would be very frightened. I frequently went to Paris with her and her sister, and the three of us visited cinemas and bars. I had last been to Paris in 1932, and compared with the city as I had found it then, it now seemed indescribably sad.

A day or two before Christmas I met Kilburg for the first time since he had brought me to the house. He took me to see Captain Fritz, and it was the latter who outlined what had been planned for me. He began by asking me whether I would be willing to return to England.

'Certainly,' I said, 'but you must not ask or expect me to do anything which would directly lead to the death of any of my countrymen.'

Fritz assured me that this was well understood by his superiors. Immediately after Christmas I was to go into training. This would consist of learning a secret code, the use of secret inks, meteorological training, brushing up my Morse receiving and key operating, and so on. In order to facilitate matters I had been granted the rank of *Sonderführer*, which is roughly equivalent to Acting-Lieutenant, in the Luftwaffe. There was, however, one great difficulty, which seemed to be insurmountable, and unless a solution could be found, the whole idea would break down.

'How are you to get possession of a radio transmitter?' Fritz asked. 'You can't take one with you, and we can't send you one. Have you any ideas?'

I had already given a good deal of thought to this, but now I pretended to think it over once more; then I said with some uncertainty:

'My training in England consisted of taking down and reassembling various types of transmitters. If you could get me a simple circuit which I could learn by heart, I think I could make a set in England.'

'How would you get the parts?' Fritz asked.

'It used to be possible, before the war, to buy spare

parts in junk shops quite easily. I could get all the parts I should need without creating any suspicion. The greatest snag would be frequency crystals; but I believe there's a method of overcoming this difficulty by using coils. But I should need special instruction in how to make them.'

Fritz thought over this suggestion for a while, then agreed that Hugo should test me. It will be appreciated, I think, how deeply I had to identify myself with the character I was playing. I had to become at one and the same time a treacherous agent and an officer and an English gentleman. We were acting from an unwritten script, and I did not know the lines of those who were playing opposite me until they were spoken, so it sometimes required a very quick wit to frame satisfactory answers. There were two possible pit-falls. First, I should certainly be out of character as an English gentleman if I appeared too eager to act as a traitor: second, if my eagerness to impress my treachery on the Germans did not carry deep ideological conviction, I should immediately be suspect. Fortunately my circumstances allowed me enough time to consider very carefully every movement that I made. But I had to keep my wits very much about me in personal contacts, so as to reply spontaneously and in keeping with my character.

On the afternoon of Christmas Eve we exchanged presents round a small Christmas tree. Next day the Hugos went to visit Simone, Hugo's sister. That afternoon I was playing two-handed patience with Gaston, the maid's lover, when he suddenly said, apparently *à propos* of nothing:

'You are an Englishman, aren't you M. Reynaud?' – this was the name used for me, as a varient of Ronny.

I can only hope I didn't look as stunned as I felt. All I could do on the spur of the moment was to answer him quizzically, as though I thought he meant it as a joke.

'And what makes you ask that?' I enquired.

He shrugged his shoulders. 'One can always tell, Monsieur,' he said. 'You are not a collaborator either. You are playing some sort of game – a dangerous game, I think. But you may trust Lucille and me. If you ever need any help, don't hesitate to ask. It would give me great pleasure to have my revenge on Madame.'

I desperately wanted to pursue the conversation, but I did not dare. Though I knew that no love was lost between Mme Hugo and Gaston and Lucille, I had no proof of where the sympathies of these two really lay. Later on, however, I was to discover that what he had told me was true enough.

When the Hugos returned that evening Madame Hugo said to me triumphantly, 'Dr Kilburg has given permission for you to go out walking alone in the Bois, as long as you tell us when you are going.'

It was like the glimpse of the sun that I had had on my

birthday, this first sign that I was gaining Kilburg's confidence. I had not dared to hope that I should achieve results so soon.

On December 28th the Hugos went with Simone and Doctor Kilburg to the Haute Savoie by car, the two men to visit agents, the women going along for the ride. I was left alone with Lucille, Gaston and the old cook, Bette. This was the opportunity I had been hoping for, and it gave me a chance to consult Hugo's radio books. I also studied very carefully every paper and document that I could find, some of which were highly confidential. I shall refer later to the events of these few days, for they saw the beginning of a collaboration between Madame Lupin and myself which showed a courage on her part that has never been recognised or appreciated, either by her own countrymen or mine.

My training began early in January but during the next few months it was to prove very erratic. Under Hugo's guidance I revised my Morse, and learned how to convert an ordinary commercial radio receiver into a transmitter. I made two such sets, which enabled him to report to Fritz that our greatest difficulty had been overcome.

Sometimes weeks went by without my seeing or hearing from anyone. I suggested to Hugo that I should write to Kilburg, but he advised me strongly against doing so, as it might easily enrage the unpredictable Doctor, and then I should quickly find myself back in Frankfurt.

Towards the end of the month an elderly captain of the Wehrmacht, wearing civilian clothes, appeared and began to teach me the use of the latest German secret ink. As he spoke neither English nor French, a young Luftwaffe lieutenant in the Doctor's service accompanied him as interpreter. He introduced himself as Dr Krauss. After a few minutes' conversation we discovered that we had been contempories at Cambridge, he at King's and myself at Peterhouse. Shortly after this, Fritz was posted from Paris and Krauss was then put in charge of my training. This association with him showed me clearly why the German Secret Service, in spite of carrying its security precautions to fantastic lengths, was, in fact, extremely 'insecure'.

It was officially forbidden for members of the Intelligence services to have liaisons with Frenchwomen. Yet Krauss, who was quartered at the Hotel Scribe, also kept a flat, which I visited several times to receive instruction in the kind of military intelligence that the Germans would require from me when I returned to England, and on each occasion Krauss reclined on a couch with his head in the lap of his mistress, an extremely beautiful young actress. Krauss assured me that she spoke nothing but French, but once when I got there before he had arrived, I had a long conversation with her in English. What her position was I do not know, but French Intelligence must have had an easy task if they employed many agents like her. On another occasion Krauss had a telephone conversation with me on the ordinary open line about the use of certain codes. Then I was suddenly told that he had disappeared, and that was the last I ever heard of him.

Presently I began to receive meteorological instruction from a very pleasant and cultured German with whom I went for walks in the Bois, the Tuileries Gardens or the Luxembourg while we studied the skies. In the evenings we sat on the boulevards discussing philosophy and politics.

In the middle of March I decided that I would risk writing to Kilburg, as I wanted to point out that the operation which was contemplated held a considerable risk for me. If I were caught by the British I would immediately be shot as a traitor, in which case my property would be annexed by the Crown. To provide for my family, should this happen, I requested the payment of £5,000 sterling, which sum I would deposit with a trusted friend who would invest it for my family if anything went wrong.

By this time the R.A.F.'s raids on the industrial suburbs of Paris were beginning to be stepped up, and bombs were beginning to fall too near the house for Madame Hugo's peace of mind; so now she began to agitate for a move to a safer place. After some difficulty she found a small villa at Meudon about seven miles north of Paris.

The necessary arrangements were soon made, and just after Easter we moved in.

Near the villa lived M. Raoul Charpentier and his wife. He was an official at Radio Paris and had made frequent visits to England and America, and spoke English well. Mme Charpentier was a fearless Anglophile. She knew of Hugo's connection with the Germans and she knew that his wife was a dangerous woman; yet I heard her say repeatedly in the presence of both of them how delighted she would be when the English arrived in Paris.

During my stay at Meudon-val-Fleury I was to see a good deal of the Charpentiers, and that I have been able to preserve this account of my adventures is in no small part due to M. Charpentier's courage and resource.

CHAPTER 13

MADAME LUPIN

THÉRÈSE Lupin shared a flat with a Mme Renée Bernard and her son Charles. She had been married when she was fifteen, had two daughters, and was divorced at the age of twenty. At the beginning of the war she had served as a nurse in a military hospital at Lyons. While she was there she was arrested on suspicion of being a German spy, but was later released when investigations showed that the suspicions were unfounded. When France collapsed she returned to Paris, and as the Hugos were at that time penniless, she supported not only them but Hugo's sister Simone.

Thérèse was a strikingly beautiful woman, dark, *chic* and not unlike the *femme fatale* of spy fiction; a fact which was doubtless responsible for her troubles with the counter-espionage authorities. On the arrival of the Germans, shortly after Kilburg had made contact with Hugo, the Doctor had used every resource to persuade her to work for him, but she rejected his suggestions, so he desisted, apparently without bearing her any grudge.

Mme Hugo was resentful of her sister's attitude to Kilburg, which she doubtless felt would jeopardise her own relations with the Germans, and she developed an *idée fixe* that Thérèse was in the pay of the English. Although she still professed to love Thérèse deeply, she became, in fact, her most dangerous enemy.

In 1942 Mme Hugo, aided and abetted by Simone, had proved her hatred of her sister by denouncing her to the Gestapo as a British agent. But the Gestapo were unable to prove anything against her and she was set free. Knowing that Simone hated her, chiefly because of her good looks, Thérèse forgave Mme Hugo, whom she believed to be completely under Simone's influence.

On the day the Hugos set out for their trip to the Haute Savoie, Mme Hugo had given Lucille and Gaston permission to spend New Year's Day with relations on the other side of Paris, which left only old Bette to look after me. She had never got on well with Lucille and Gaston and, shortly after they had left, Bette obviously much upset, came to me and said, 'I'm going! I won't stand this any longer.'

What it was that she wouldn't stand wasn't very clear, but all the remonstrations in the world would not stop her, and away she went. Thus I was left with the villa to myself, which suited me very well. It gave me a magnificent opportunity to ransack the whole house without fear of being caught. Much that I had not discovered during my previous search was now revealed to me, giving a complete picture of Hugo's activities.

Late in the afternoon I set off for Paris, where I had tea and then went to a cinema. At the Pont de Neuilly metro station a German soldier, who I imagine was either mad or drunk, suddenly and without the slightest provocation pulled out his revolver and fired at me. I felt a sharp pain in my right buttock. Thinking it would be wiser not to enquire too closely into what was going on, I started to run. Immediately other people began to follow me, but it was dark by this time and when I had managed to shake off my pursuers I went into a café and ordered a cognac. Feeling in my hip pocket for some money, I withdrew my hand and found that it was smeared with blood. I swallowed my cognac quickly and made my way home.

Back at the villa, I went upstairs to the bedroom and stripped off my clothes, for the wound, though not much more than a graze, was bleeding fairly freely. Leaving my clothes in a heap on the floor, I went into the bathroom to staunch the blood. I was sitting on the edge of the bath with my back to the door, when suddenly I heard the voice of Thérèse behind me.

'What on earth has happened, Reynaud?'

I told her, and she immediately fetched some dressings from her sister's bedroom and strapped up the wound.

Presently I began to tremble violently; the reaction, I suppose, of delayed shock. Thérèse noticing this, sent me to bed at once and went downstairs to prepare some food. While I was eating it, she suddenly said to me:

'Why are you Englishmen so mad?' I was so taken by surprise that I could say nothing. 'It's all right,' she went on. 'You couldn't be anything but an Englishman. But you needn't be afraid. I am a hundred per cent Anglophile.'

When Mme Hugo subsequently realised that my acquaintance with Thérèse was becoming more friendly, she created scenes of jealousy. It was necessary to go warily, for I realised that Mme Hugo's constant abuse of her sister was quite likely to result in a fresh denunciation to the Germans. When I tried to impress this upon Thérèse, she would not believe me, although Charles Bernard, who knew the Hugos well, strongly supported me. Eventually Mme Hugo's behaviour became so insupportable that I told Hugo I thought she was behaving very foolishly. Not unexpectedly, he supported her and added that I should discontinue seeing Thérèse.

Gaston and Lucille could hardly avoid knowing what was going on, for Mme Hugo had a shrill and uncontrollable voice when she was angry. Now they began to do all they could to help me. Gaston carried notes to Thérèse, and Marie, her cook, brought me replies. Using my meteorologist instructor as an excuse, I went often to her flat, for such visits had become essential to me. I could never have supported the heavy strain of all these months of watching tongue and action if it had not been for the comfort and kindness, and above all, the complete relaxation which I found there. Mme Bernard and her son were entirely pro-Ally, and while Charles was cautious, his mother was completely outspoken. If this part of my operation can be adjudged successful, it is very largely due to Thérése.

At this time I began to feel that my own affairs were not going well. The letter I had sent to Kilburg had infuriated him, as Hugo had predicted; and now he threatened to send me back to Frankfurt if I bothered him any more.

I therefore decided to try to find some way of escape. The concièrge of Madame Lupin's house had a brother who had escaped to England via Brest, and her sister-in-law knew the contacts who arranged such things. So the concièrge was taken into our confidence, and wrote to her sister-in-law. In the meantime Charles Bernard made plans for getting me to Brest. He provided the necessary money for my wants, bought the tickets and insisted that he would accompany me to the outskirts of Brest, so that my accent should not betray me.

Before the concièrge's sister-in-law could reply, we had moved to Meudon, and three days after we arrived Hugo said to me:

'The Doctor has asked me to tell you that he has just

been informed by the Berlin authorities that they will not consent to your operation. They say that you are either a very clever actor or a fanatic. Neither is of any use in this job; so they have ordered your return to Frankfurt.'

I was so overcome that for some moments I felt physically sick and wanted to rush from the room. Then I realised that this decision had been made without anyone from Berlin having seen me. However, I could do nothing but accept defeat. I wondered how soon they would take me back to Frankfurt and whether I would have time to get away to Brest before this happened.

Then Hugo went on: 'The Doctor still has great confidence in you. He believes you are sincere, and wants to help you; so he has asked another Service if they can use you. A Monsieur Fabré from this Service is coming to see you tomorrow morning.'

I knew now that I should have to begin all over again. Perhaps it would not be quite so difficult this time, for surely, I thought, Kilburg's report on me would help a little. I decided that I would carry on with the Brest idea all the same, in case the new possibility should also fall through. But obviously, if I returned to England in this way, it would be without inks or radio contacts, concerning both of which I knew that any information I could bring back would be invaluable.

At ten o'clock next morning, M. Fabré arrived with

the meteorologist as interpreter. Fabré was one of the handsomest men I have seen. He asked me many searching questions, and at the end of two hours said:

'Don't worry. I'll work it out somehow. There is one thing, though, that would make it an absolute certainty — hostages for your good faith. Is there anyone over here, a relation of some sort, who would act as security for you?'

I said of course, that there was no one.

On the Monday following Fabré's visit, I had arranged a rendezvous with Thérèse, who, seeing that I was more than ordinarily preoccupied, pressed me to tell her the reason. Eventually I told her about the interview with Fabré and his final question.

At once she said, 'I will be a hostage for you.'

I naturally dismissed the idea as utterly impossible, but she refused to listen to reason, and after a long argument I said at last that I would think it over. I knew that even if I had not liked and respected her as much as I did, it would have been impossible for me to place her in a position of such danger. And yet, as I continued to think it over, I wondered whether I would be justified in not accepting such an offer, which she had made with her eyes wide open, when refusal would prevent my doing a valuable service to my country.

Presently, however, I began to see a possible solution.

If I could persuade Fabré to agree, and could make an arrangement whereby Thérèse would be left at liberty, provided she reported to the Gestapo every day, I believed it might be possible to deceive the Germans long enough to get her safely hidden away somewhere, or, better still, brought to England. Having reached this conclusion, I told her when I saw her on Wednesday that I was going to accept her offer. In order not to raise false hopes, however, I said nothing about my intention to try to get her protected.

The following day I met Fabré and explained the position to him. I said that Thérèse and I were great friends, and I felt sure that if she were asked she would readily become a hostage for me. Naturally, I said, I had not spoken to her yet, because I wanted to know what he thought of the proposal. Mme Lupin believed me to be a Finn; she did not know what I was doing, and could simply be told that I was undertaking special work for Germany, the nature of which was extremely delicate and required me to offer some sort of personal guarantee of my integrity. I suggested my tentative plan for her to report daily to the Gestapo, and Fabré approved of this. He said, however, that before he gave a definite answer, he would like to see her for himself. I therefore arranged for a meeting in her flat. This took place soon afterwards and when it was over Fabré declared himself satisfied.

* * *

As May drew to a close, things in Paris were becoming more and more uncomfortable. The Metro ran for only a few hours every day; the gas was only turned on for a quarter of an hour at seven-thirty in the morning, for half an hour at half-past twelve; and again for half an hour at seven in the evening — and when it was on there was practically no pressure. The electric current was switched on at half-past eleven in the evening, and off again at half-past five in the morning. At half-past nine, when it became too dark to see indoors, Paris went to bed; and the birth-rate rose proportionately with the hours of darkness. Food was becoming scarce, owing to the breakdown of communications, and the French were growing increasingly despondent about the chances of a second front.

June 5th being my thirty-third birthday, Thérèse had arranged a special luncheon, to which Fabré had been invited. At five minutes to one his secretary telephoned to say that he would be unable to come, as he had an unexpected engagement.

Throughout the day there was an almost continuous alert, and the Metro was running very infrequently. At half-past six in the evening, when I left for the Gare des Invalides to catch the train to Meudon, the Metro was shut, and when I telephoned the station I was told that no more trains would leave for Meudon until tomorrow.

So I then telephoned to Hugo and told him I would be staying in Paris overnight with Fabré.

It so happened that at this time an uncle of Hugo's, called Ludwig Werner, who knew Mme Lupin, was stationed at the Naval H.Q. in the Avenue Montaigne. He was a strange character, morose, seldom sober and a menace when he was drunk. He was very fond of Thérèse and jealous of any man to whom she showed even the ordinary social courtesies. He had created several scenes because of my friendship with her, and had warned her that I was a 'filthy Englishman'; Mme Hugo, in direct contravention of Kilburg's instructions, having told him my nationality.

This evening Werner came in for a drink, and immediately there was another scene. Firmly but politely – though perhaps a little unwisely, for this time he was sober – I put him out of the flat. At the time, I thought no more about the incident, though it was to have its repercussions later on.

The next morning when I woke up and switched on the radio beside my bed I was stunned for a few minutes by what I heard. Then I realised that the Second Front, for which all France had been waiting so long, had actually begun.

It is difficult to describe that day. In the streets people seemed calm, though not particularly hopeful, curbing their enthusiasm until they saw how things would go. Many, indeed, were sceptical, for German propaganda about the impregnability of the Atlantic Wall had been very successful. Owing to the shortage of official news – and what little there was was controlled by the enemy – a wild crop of rumours began to circulate immediately. A few intrepid patriots publicly declared their sympathies with the Allies, and were shot by the Germans on the spot.

Fabré, whom I saw again in the afternoon, told me he was shortly going to Berlin to press forward final arrangements for my operation. In view of the new development – by this he meant the invasion – he thought it would be better that I should leave Meudon, chiefly because of the difficulty of getting to and fro. He was hoping to persuade his Paris chief to approve my coming to live there. Meanwhile he instructed me to return to Meudon and said he would send a car for me the following day to bring my belongings to Paris.

That evening I dined with Thérèse. Werner was there again, more silent and morose than ever. Nevertheless, there was an atmosphere of festivity about the dinner table, for Mme Bernard could not restrain her joy, and even though she knew it was dangerous, she did not hesitate to put her hopes into words.

When the salad was served, she apologised for the absence of oil, and without considering what I was saying, I said, 'Never mind: when the English arrive in Paris there

will be plenty.' It was a stupid thing to say, and I soon had
cause to regret it.

At eight o'clock I caught the train for Meudon, and
when I arrived I found the Hugos on the point of setting
out for a conference with Kilburg. What plans they made
that night I do not know, but it was long after midnight
when they came back.

The invasion, of course, raised all those doubts in my
mind that had been constantly with me since I had first
contemplated escaping to Brest. I still had the opportunity; I had the money – provided by Charles Bernard and
Thérèse – and I felt sure I could find somewhere to hide
until the Allies arrived; but this again would have meant
returning home almost empty-handed – and Fabré would
have Thérèse as a hostage.

On his return from Paris, Hugo gave me a message
from Fabré, saying that I should not be fetched until after
the week-end. Early on Friday morning, he and Madame
Hugo went to Paris to collect as much money as they
could lay hands on, leaving me alone in the villa.

Since coming to Meudon I had had my eye on a wardrobe
in the Hugos' bedroom, for it was the only cupboard in the
whole house that was always locked. This time, however,
the key had been left in the door, and before long I was
looking through a large pile of documents which were inside.
As I went through them, I carefully noted the position of

each one and the order they were in, so that I could return them without showing that they had been touched. I went through every paper. The majority were copies of reports from the hundreds of German agents hidden throughout France, giving information of local conditions and dangers. Then, in an envelope concealed among the pages of one of these reports, I found what I was looking for. About four months before, I had discovered that Hugo had received a new code, which was being distributed to many of the German agents because the one they had previously been using had been compromised. On several occasions I had tried unsuccessfully to get particulars of this code. Now at last I had it in front of me.

I went downstairs and got a scrap of tissue paper, then copied the code on to it, sign by sign. Afterwards I returned the envelope and papers to the wardrobe.

It had been decided by Fabré that I should return to England in what remained of the operational clothes I had worn when I set out. So I now took my storm-jacket to Mme Charpentier, who unpicked two seams, fixed the minute rolls of paper inside, and then sewed the seams up again with her sewing-machine.

When the Hugos returned from Paris, they had Thérèse with them, whom they had invited for the week-end. Madame Hugo was most affectionate towards her, never addressing her except with endearments.

Monday came, and I waited all day for Fabré's friends, but they didn't turn up. The next morning I was still in my dressing-gown when two men arrived at the villa and told me to get ready. What it was about them, I don't know, but from the moment that I saw them I was filled with uneasiness, and as I began to pack, this premonition grew stronger.

Thérèse was still in bed when I went into her room to say goodbye.

'Don't be afraid,' I whispered. 'Trust me always. I believe they are taking me back to prison.'

She sat up horrified.

'You must escape,' she said. 'Go through the window. There is money in my handbag – thirty thousand francs. I'll keep them guessing.'

By this time Madame Hugo was calling me from the foot of the stairs: the two men were becoming impatient.

'It's too late,' I whispered. '*Au revoir*, and thank you with all my heart.'

Downstairs in the living-room Madame Hugo had opened a bottle of champagne. It was the crowning act of her hypocrisy. She knew, as I have since discovered, where I was going; but she raised her glass to my good fortune.

CHAPTER 14

THE CHERCHE MIDI

I

WE drove to Paris in silence. There were few people about in the streets, as was usual in those days, and here and there at strategic points German soldiers were still feverishly working on concrete block-houses. Eventually we came to the Seine. As we were crossing the Pont au Change, one of my escorts asked:

'Has Dr Kilburg or M. Fabré spoken to you?'

'I haven't seen the Doctor for two months,' I said, 'nor M. Fabré for a week. He told me then he was hurrying through the final preparations for my operation.'

'I see,' said my companion. Then there was silence again.

Away on my right, as we approached the Ile de la Cité, I could see the old prison known as the Concièrgerie, and I wondered if this was to be my destination. But we went over on to the left bank of the river, crossed the Boulevard St Germain and then turned into the Rue du Cherche Midi. While we were going along my escort resumed the conversation.

'The Chief has decided that in view of the invasion it wouldn't be safe to leave you at large among the French;

219

something might easily happen to you. So we're taking you to a military prison for two or three days, till we can arrange transport for you to go to Germany and complete your training. In about two weeks you should be on your way to England.'

The Cherche Midi prison had a notorious reputation, even before the war. The Germans, who had taken it over chiefly for political prisoners, had done their best to clean it up, but they could not do much. I was entered in the records as Sven Paasikivi, and given strict instructions to speak to nobody. Before being taken to my cell, the escort who had acted as spokesman suddenly adopted a bullying attitude and demanded that I should write a letter to Thérèse at his dictation. The gist of what I wrote was roughly this:

My dear Thérèse, I have been ordered by the Finnish Government to return at once to Finland. I am leaving from the Gare de l'Est at midday, so I shan't have an opportunity to say goodbye. Will you forgive me? I will come back as soon as I can. I shall never be able to thank you for everything that you have done for me and for all your kind-ness.

Good luck, *chèrie*,
Reynaud

The cell to which I was taken measured about ten feet in each direction. It contained an iron bedstead with a straw mattress, a pillow and two blankets, both stinking and stiff with dirt. On a shelf above the bed was a chipped enamel wash-basin, a mug, a plate, a bowl, a water-jug and a spoon. On the floor was a container with a lid; it was lined with the excreta of former inmates.

On the roof of the prison immediately above my cell was an air-raid siren. The R.A.F. was now raiding Paris several times every twenty-four hours, and as the French warning system had a pre-alert, an alert, a pre-all-clear and then an all-clear, the effect on the nerves can well be imagined.

Reveille was at eight o'clock, and at nine a mug of ersatz coffee was distributed: this was our breakfast. Thereafter the meals were little different from those at Dulag West. At five o'clock tables, stools, spoon, braces and boots were put outside the cell door, to be taken in at reveille next morning. By five-past five all prisoners were in bed for the night. On Sunday reveille was at nine, coffee at nine-thirty, soup at eleven-thirty, and bread and tea at noon. Tables, stools and the rest were put out at twelve-thirty, and at twelve-thirty-five came bed. This arrangement applied also to Saturday afternoons. I was allowed three French novels a week, and twenty cigarettes. We were exercised once every ten days for a period of twenty minutes, shaved twice a week, and allowed one cold shower a month.

It is generally held by experts that bed-bugs emerge only at night. Those at the Cherche Midi were not so particular; they came out whenever they wished, during the day as well as during the night. They were loathsome, swollen things as big as your fingernail and transparent, except when they were puffed with human blood; when they were killed they emitted a sickening, sweet stench. At night they kept me awake by scuttling up and down my body. For one who abominates all creeping things, as I do, it was an ordeal so revolting as to be past belief. Fortunately I had been allowed to keep a pair of pyjamas, though in a few days they were stiff with dirt from the filthy blanket. Nor did they prevent my developing a severe attack of scabies, which covered the whole of my body with tiny eruptions.

After a week had gone by without any message from Fabré, I realised that I had been trapped. It was the end of all my plans; all the anxieties of the last eight months, all my endeavours to turn my initial failure into some sort of success had come to nothing. The strain of these past months and the acute disappointment of finding myself once more a prisoner deprived me of all heart. At Tallinn, at Riga, and at Frankfurt I had refused to submit; but now I let my nerves take what toll they demanded. My morale sank to zero. I did not bother to wash, my hair became matted, my clothes stained and creased; it was no use carrying on. From my shelf a photograph of Thérèse mocked at my cowardice and lack of manhood. Then, when fourteen days had passed, I demanded pen and paper and wrote to Fabré.

A day or two later he came to see me.

'The operation is off,' he said. Although in my heart I had known all along that this was so, it was a bitter blow to hear it confirmed at last.

'I can do nothing,' Fabré went on. 'You have only your own stupidity to thank.'

'But why?' I asked. 'Why have you suddenly lost confidence in me?'

'I haven't,' he answered. 'But I can do nothing. I ought not to tell you this and it mustn't go any further. On the day after the *débarquement*' – by this he meant what we knew as D-Day – 'you dined at Mme Lupin's with Ludwig Werner. At dinner you said to Mme Bernard that it will be better when the English arrive in Paris.'

'But that's absolutely fantastic!' I said.

'I agree,' said Fabré. 'I cannot believe you would have been so stupid. However, Werner reported it to the Gestapo. He happens to have a high Party number, and has powerful friends in Berlin. After his denunciation of you, my Service wouldn't dare to go on with your operation.'

'Well, what's to happen to me?' I asked.

He stood up and went to the cell door. Then shrugged his shoulders. 'You will be returned to Germany for court-martial, and, I suppose, executed.'

So I was back where I had started. Now that it was in black and white, so to speak, I again began seriously to consider suicide; but I had no means of doing away with myself, except my pyjama cord, and that broke at the first attempt. As my mental condition deteriorated once more, my physical condition very soon grew worse; the scabies and bed-bugs drove me almost crazy at night and the hunger-pangs were as bad as they ever had been. I soon began to stink, and was not allowed to change my shirt or underclothes, although I had a change of clothing in my suitcase, which was in the prison store.

Presently I gave up even trying to read. I could not concentrate well enough to follow the sense of a line of print. All day long I sat gazing listlessly at nothing, hearing vague sounds and just managing to co-ordinate my mind and body sufficiently well to stand up when the cell door was opened.

Every morning, to keep a tally of the days, I scratched a mark on the wall. There were forty-three scratches, making the date July 25th, when I was fetched from my cell to a waiting-room in the main part of the prison. To my great surprise I found Dr Kilburg there with the meteorologist.

Both were extremely shocked by my appearance and manner, and Kilburg almost wept. The meteorologist, who for some reason seemed to be acting as spokesman for the Doctor said, 'The Doctor has asked me to explain that the authorities have demanded your return to Germany at once. You will realise, of course, that that can have only one conclusion for you.'

'It is a conclusion that I should welcome,' I said.

'Nevertheless, there is still one hope. The Doctor has found someone else who he thinks may be able to help you. You won't be able to return to England, but we could at least save your life. He is here now, if you would like to speak to him.'

I could not answer for a moment. What was the good of going through it all again? – of scheming to gain somebody else's confidence, when the authorities in Berlin, who had never even set eyes on me, were always the ones who had the last word, and the word was always 'no'? Yet hope is proverbial where there is life: and so it was that I met Count Cristopher Dönhoff.

We talked for some time, the Count sounding me about my past, my background and my political feelings. Finally, he made me a proposition.

'I belong,' he said, 'to the Political Department of the *Sicherheitsdienst* [this was the German Security Service]. I am also on the Staff of the German Foreign Office. The S.D.

and the Foreign Office are planning a *rapprochement*, or at least an understanding, between Germany and England. One of the things we must know about is the climate of political opinion in England. This is not so easy to find out though; few Englishmen seem to know what they think politically. We have many thousands of Englishmen in our prisoner of war camps. But when we talk to them they suspect a trick; they won't give us their true views. What I am going to suggest to you is that we should put you in an *Offizierslager* and that you should talk to the prisoners and from time to time send us reports. We have several other men in mind for this, but now that I have spoken to you I think that with your background you would do the job very well – better, I am sure, than most of our other candidates.'

I replied that I would like him to know at once that I would never agree to anything which would endanger the lives of other Englishmen.

'I will give you my word, as one gentleman to another, which I am sure you will accept, that I would never ask you to do anything which might do that. All I want is to get a picture of the political reaction of Englishmen. We believe that politically there has been a great change of heart in England. Although, so far as we can tell, young conservatives adopt a quasi-socialist programme, we believe the days of conservative rule are probably over. But we would like to know more. After the war England

and Germany must become allies to fight the rising tide of communism; and to do this effectively, we must have a common basis of opinion. What we are asking you to do would endanger no one's life.'

I answered that I would like to think over his proposition. Then I went back to my cell. It seemed to me that with my espionage training, it would be safer to do what Count Dönhoff suggested, than risk being handed back to the Gestapo, since I might still find ways and means of discomforting the Germans. I believed also that if I could play my cards properly, I might yet be able to devise some way of getting my information home. Yet it was only with the greatest reluctance that I overcame my inclinations. My physical and mental conditions rebelled against a continuation of the struggle. As I had told the meteorologist quite truthfully, I would have welcomed death.

When the Count visited me the following Thursday I gave him my answer. He seemed well pleased with it and went away to make arrangements for getting me out of the Cherche Midi immediately.

II

On July 29th, accompanied by Kilburg, Dönhoff returned to fetch me. During the seven weeks I had spent in the Cherche Midi I had degenerated almost into an animal. Now this trend had to be reversed, and as a first stage in my rehabilitation Dönhoff took me to an S.S. Hospital in the Place Bois de Boulogne to be cured of my scabies and to be built up again. At the entrance to the hospital I said goodbye to Kilburg, whom I thanked warmly for all his efforts on my behalf. What his motives were I never had the remotest idea and I still do not understand. I watched him drive away and that was the last time I ever saw him.

The hospital was a temporary one in a large private house which stood in a pleasant garden overlooking the Bois. It would have been pleasanter still, but for the barbed-wire coils and the block-house by which it was defended.

I was put to bed in a room on the first floor, and when the Count returned in the evening, bringing me books, cigarettes and a cigarette-lighter (since matches were almost unobtainable) he told me that he was leaving the next morning for a fortnight's visit to Berlin. During that time he wanted me to get as much fresh air and sunlight as possible and to eat well. He had bribed the French women attendants, he said, to give me extra food whenever possible, and had ordered that I was to be given a glass of wine every day for lunch and supper. Before he left, he gave me 2000 francs and returned my Paasikivi identity card.

The weather was hot and sunny, and besides four-hourly baths and applications of liniment, Dr Fritz, who was in charge of the hospital, prescribed sun-ray treatment, so that I spent most of the day lying naked on a rug in the garden.

By judicious tipping with the money which Dönhoff had given me, I soon made friends with the women attendants, joking with them, and helping them in small ways with their duties. In return, they brought me cigarettes and newspapers, and, since all the French love a lover, they posted, unknown to the Germans, two letters which I wrote to Thérèse, believing them to be *billets doux*.

As I guessed that Thérèse's mail might be censored, I enclosed my envelopes in others addressed to the concièrge of her apartment, whom I knew I could trust. I did not tell Thérèse where I was, since it would have been dangerous for her to write or come to see me. I said that I had been in prison after being denounced by Werner, and hinted that my plans were changed. I implored her to leave Paris at once and to go into the country and await the arrival of the Allies, as I was pretty sure there would soon be trouble in Paris.

By now, convinced that the liberation of the city would be a matter of a few weeks at most, and not knowing what might happen to me, I decided that I would try to leave behind a report for my superiors, in the hope that it would reach them in time to do some good, and also to give an account of what I had been doing with myself. Among my few possessions, I had a foolscap notebook containing sixty or seventy pages; so for the next week I wrote an account of some thirty thousand words, covering the period from October 24th, 1942 to August 7th, 1944. I ran little risk in the actual writing of it, for, except when I was in the garden, no one came near me except Dr Fritz, who only appeared occasionally. My report included full particulars of the code I had stolen from Hugo, for I still had the copy on tissue paper which Mme Charpentier had sewn into the seams of my storm-jacket.

When I had finished the report I sent it through the post to M. Charpentier at Radio Paris. It was a great risk for both of us; if the envelope were opened in the post, it would reveal me in my true colours; for M. Charpentier it would mean death. I had absolute confidence in him, however, and I knew that if he received it, he would do as I asked. The worst thing was that I could never know if it had reached him, since it would not be safe for him to reply to me, as I knew that any letters I might get would be censored. In my mind, the risk of discovery, even though it involved some risk to M. Charpentier's life, was justifiable; for if my report got through, it would present my superiors with a considerable amount of valuable information.

I finished writing my report on the afternoon of August 9th, and gave it to one of the French women to post. On August 16th, rumours which had been wild before, grew wilder. The Allies were said to have landed in the south, Grenoble had fallen, Allied tanks were in Chartres, and Allied paratroops had descended on Versailles. There were no newspapers, Paris was cut off from all communication with the rest of France, and as the controlled radio gave accounts of German victories, which no one could accept, it was impossible to know what to believe.

The Place Bois de Boulogne was given over to the S.S. There were only two entrances to the Place, and these were guarded by S.S. troops, block-houses and barriers. To get in or out it was necessary to show not only one's identity card, but a special pass. For the last two or three days, S.S. troops from houses nearby had been feeding a large bonfire in our garden with papers, which they heaped on to it for hours on end. All day long we could see Allied aircraft flying over Paris at will. It was clear that the situation for the Germans was becoming very serious.

On the evening of the 16th the rumour went round that the hospital was to be evacuated. Again I was faced with the question of what I should do. I was practically certain that I could evade the guards, and if I could get into Paris, I felt pretty sure I could find somewhere to hide. But supposing the rumours were not true? Supposing Thérèse had not left Paris and was still at Fabré's mercy? Supposing . . . supposing . . .

I was still trying to make up my mind what to do when

I was told that Dr Fritz would like me to take coffee with him in the garden. This was an innovation, which I thought might be because he had something important to tell me.

So far, in spite of the rumours, the hospital was quiet; there were no signs of preparation for a move and everything seemed normal. As we sat under a big tree in the garden the air-raid sirens began to sound; soon we could see formations of the R.A.F. twinkling like many moving stars in the evening sunlight against a dark blue sky. A few minutes later we heard the crump of their bombs, but flak opposition was negligible, and there was no need even to take cover.

After I had drunk my first cup of coffee, Dr Fritz excused himself for a moment. Suddenly without any warning I began to feel hopelessly drowsy. Sweat broke out all over my body and I could breathe only with difficulty. My first thought was that I had been poisoned. I couldn't speak; I wanted to be sick, with a feeling of nausea deep down in the pit of my stomach. Somehow I pulled myself to my feet, and staggered up to my room, panting violently. I threw off my shirt and trousers which were all I had on, and fell naked on to my bed. As I did so the whole room started to swim and I passed out.

CHAPTER 15

IN RETREAT

I WAS awakened by someone shaking me by the shoulder. It was still daylight. My head was burning and I felt as though a weight were clamped to the back of my neck, preventing me from raising myself. Although I could not focus my eyes properly, I could see Count Dönhoff bending over me. He was calling me urgently.

'Get up and put your things together and come down quickly! We must be off in five minutes.'

When he was satisfied that I was properly awake, he went away and an orderly came in to pack my few things.

'What's the time?' I asked him.

'Eight o'clock.'

'Have I only slept five minutes then?' I said.

'You've been asleep all night.'

'All night? You mean it's eight o'clock in the morning?'

I made an effort to spring off the bed, but my head swam and I felt top-heavy. I got into the bathroom and doused my head, then shaved and dressed as quickly as I could. As I went downstairs I saw that all the rooms were empty and the mattresses and blankets gone from the beds.

233

'What's happened?' I asked the orderly, who was behind me.

'Evacuation during the night.'

The whole hospital had been evacuated, and I had heard nothing. I knew then that Dr Fritz had drugged my coffee so that I should not escape during the confusion. I presume, though I never found out, that he had had no instructions about what to do with me and did not want to take the responsibility of carting me along with him.

Outside in the Place I found Dönhoff with a garrulous Frenchman, who was explaining to him the various gauges on the dashboard of a Bugatti. As we drove off in it, Dönhoff told me what had happened.

'We are likely to see an American tank at any moment. They've broken through, and we can't hold them. All our communications have broken down, and we can get no definite news.'

We drove to the Avenue Flandin, the Headquarters of the Political Department of the *Sicherheitsdienst* in France. Half a dozen armed S.S. troops were on guard at each end of the street, inspecting the identity cards and passes of everyone who entered or left it. A string of lorries stood in front of the house.

I followed Dönhoff to a room on the third floor and waited while he shaved and tidied himself, for he had arrived from Berlin at 4 a.m. As I waited by the window I watched the scene down in the street, wondering whether I ought to make an attempt to get away. But the guards were being too thorough, and there were far too many of them for anyone without papers to attempt to get through.

The *Herrenvolk*, armed to the teeth with revolvers, rifles, knives and bayonets, some in field-dress, some in full dress, privates and generals alike were hustling about, everyone with a suitcase or a bag. The street was one where wealthy Parisians had once lived, and the fittings and furnishings of the house used as Headquarters were luxurious and in exquisite taste. The S.S. men were looting it as fast as they could load the lorries which were drawn up outside. I went downstairs with Dönhoff and watched beautiful carpets and gilded mirrors, Louis Seize chairs, and inlaid side-tables being piled into the lorries. I could not resist saying to him, as I pointed to a fine painting which two S.S. men were carrying out: 'Did this come from Berlin?'

When the lorries had been stacked, each driver took a net and fixed it so that it completely covered the lorry; then the nearby bushes and trees were stripped of their branches, which were entwined in the nets, and when everything was ready the convoy moved off.

It was an odd assortment of army trucks and private cars, loaded with all sorts of impedimenta and private belongings. In each vehicle were Germans in S.S. uniforms or in civilian clothes, accompanied by toothy, ample *Fräuleins, chic* young French girls, more discreet than valorous, French collaborators, complacent or excitable dogs of all sorts and sizes, and birds in cages.

As we passed through the streets the French looked on, curiously calm. From every avenue poured converging convoys. Going past the Palais de Chaillot, the first car fell out with engine-trouble — an accident that was to happen many times before we reached our destination. Taking the secondary roads whenever possible, to avoid attacks from the air, we arrived at the village of Coclois, where the first stop was made. Just as there were men and belongings of all sorts in the company, so there were all sorts of cars: old ones, new ones, battered two-seaters and glittering limousines, army trucks and old requisitioned lorries, fast cars, like the Bugatti in which I was travelling with Dönhoff, and antique, protesting Peugeots, from whose radiators clouds of steam issued. Between Paris and Coclois the convoy split into two parts — fast and slow. The fast would drive ahead for fifty kilometres, then pull up by the side of the road and wait for the slower vehicles to catch up.

The weather was perfect and we drove all day. It was about ten o'clock when at last we pulled up for the night at a village called Soncourt, a few miles north of Chaumont. Having found a farm with a large barn, the General requisitioned it, and somehow or other the protesting French farmer's wife was induced to provide omelettes for us. Then, exhausted, we fell into the hay and slept.

The next morning we were up early, and after a wash under the farmyard pump, and a snack of German Army biscuits and tinned beef, we began our journey again. We drove south-east through a string of villages until, at a quarter to three, we drew to a halt in Vittel, our destination.

Being in peace-time a fashionable watering-place, Vittel consists mostly of large luxury hotels. The main street was now lined with a high barbed-wire barricade, and behind it were living between two and three thousand civilian internees and their families. Walking down the street one could hear shrill Cockney voices and broad Yorkshire accents, mingling with those of Americans and Italians. Grandmothers and grandfathers, mothers and fathers, babies and adolescents, newly-weds and courting couples had lived in this confined spot for three or more years.

The hotels not occupied by the internees were accommodating the retreating S.S. The Political Department of the *Sicherheitsdienst* had been allotted the sixth floor of the Hotel Beau Site. While I guarded the Bugatti and its contents, Dönhoff skilfully staked a claim to a corner room. I appointed myself his batman, and in the seven days that followed, a relationship came into being which, in other times, might have developed into a lifelong friendship.

Cristopher Dönhoff came of an ancient Prussian family with large estates in East Prussia. Before the war he had spent ten years in Kenya, studying the conservation of big game. His English was perfect, and his French only a little less so. Whether he had been a member of the *Auslandsorganisation*, the organisation of Germans living abroad, I never discovered. I did discover his Party card, however, but the number indicated that he had joined it as a late comer. He had a very clear perception of world politics, and was not always in agreement with German policy, but he was above all a patriot and felt the shame of Germany's defeat more deeply than any other German I met. I believe he was honest, according to his lights, and was capable of deep thought and close reasoning. He was, in fact, a cultured and intelligent man in whose company it was a pleasure to be after three years of isolation. Underlying his whole nature, however, was a snobbishness peculiar to the Prussian aristocrat. I played upon this vigorously yet discreetly, and in time it helped achieve such success as I had with the S.S.

Dönhoff knew everyone of importance in German diplomatic circles, and in the S.S. From this point of view he was far more important than the General at Riga or his Chief of Staff or Bütt, Schmitt, Kilburg, or Fabré. Through him I was thrust into events entirely outside my sphere as an insignificant agent; and if it seems that I bungled my opportunities at the end, it was frankly because I was not sufficiently clever or experienced.

The news from Paris was unofficial and conflicting; news of the war was even more uncertain. The S.S. at Vittel were unable to obtain orders from their supreme H.Q., which some thought had moved to Epinal, others to Metz or to Nancy, where after four days, they were finally located.

During the next seven days Cristopher and I hammered out detailed plans for my joining a prisoner of war camp. We also worked out methods for my getting information to him, and arranged cover stories. Briefly, the information required by the S.D., so far as I can recollect it, fell under three main headings:

I. INTERNAL

(a) The Royal family

(b) Churchill

(c) Leading British statesmen with particular reference to: (i) Eden (ii) Bevin (iii) Cripps

(d) The political parties and their possible post-war policies

(e) Rehabilitation and housing

(f) Nationalisation

(g) Special reference to the Common Wealth Party

II. EXTERNAL

(a) British relations with: (i) Dominions (ii) U.S.S.R.
(iii) U.S.A. (iv) France

(b) U.S.A. relations with Europe

(c) U.S.S.R. relations with Europe

(d) U.S.A. relations with U.S.S.R.

III. GENERAL

(a) World markets

(b) World communications

(c) Oil

(d) The influence of the Church in politics

(e) The growth of the Roman Catholic Church in England

(f) The future of Germany in the event of an Allied victory.

When we were not in conference, but at meals or odd times when we were together, I began to hint that I was a rather more important person than I had wished it to be known; and so by degrees I began to sow the seeds of a cover story of my own. I would let fall casual claims to acquaintance with many famous British personages. It was really a highly developed series of variations on the stories I had invented in the Frankfurt prison for the Gestapo. There were wildly apocryphal stories of the Royal family, intimate meetings with Mr Churchill, with whom I now began to claim a close relationship – hence my interest in and knowledge of politics and foreign affairs – lunches with Mr Eden, chats with Mr Bevin, tea with Sir Stafford Cripps. Lying awake into the small hours, which was the only time I was really on my own, I worked it all out in a wealth of colourful and convincing detail.

Now that I knew what the S.D. requirements were I was able to work out my own plans for dealing with the situation. I persuaded Cristopher that I should enter the Oflag under the assumed name of Captain John de Witt, explaining that this was a rarely-used family name which would be recognised by my wife. I pointed out — with some trepidation, for on this hung my chief ambition — that I should have to write letters and receive them from home; otherwise the suspicions of the British prisoners might be aroused. It took a little persuasion to get Cristopher to agree to this, since technically I would not be a prisoner of war; but he saw the force of my argument and in the end gave way.

My method of dealing with the opinions that I was to collect was my next most important consideration. I would have to sift everything very carefully and in my presentation of the material attempt to mislead the Germans as far as possible — a course which I had followed to the best of my ability from the first day of my interrogation by Nädlinger. I was now dealing, of course, with very astute opponents, whose political acumen was obviously greater than mine. If I were extremely clever — and very fortunate

— I thought I might keep up the deception for about three months; by which time — or so I thought then — the Allies would be in Berlin. If they were not, my end would probably be a sticky one after all.

The cover story that Cristopher and I worked out, which I was to tell the officers in the camp and my superiors when I arrived home, would be true up to the time of my entering the Frankfurt prison. From then on my story was to be that I had escaped during an R.A.F. raid, jumped a freight train going to France, left it at Verdun, and made my way to Paris, where I was hidden by the Resistance. This was supposed to have happened in March, 1944. When the invasion started I decided to try to get through to the British lines: so I joined the Maquis north of Paris — it was they who had given me the British uniform I would be wearing in the camp — and after being with them for six weeks, I made an attempt to get through near Rouen. At dawn of August 27th, about a mile and a half from the British lines, I walked into a German observation post and was captured. I was taken back and passed from one German unit to another, until I was finally handed over at Coblenz.

On Sunday morning, August 27th, Cristopher and I, accompanied by two S.S. men, set out in two cars for Chalons-sur-Marne, where a large Oflag was situated. We stopped for lunch at Domremy, the village where Joan of

Arc was born, and arrived at Chalons at about six o'clock. Here we found chaos. Communications had completely broken down and no one was receiving any orders — if any were being issued. The Wehrmacht seemed paralysed when there was no one to tell it what to do. We found that all units were acting on their own initiative; which meant that they were packing up everything they could lay hands on and scurrying east. When Cristopher went out to the Oflag he found everyone had left for Germany six hours before.

Early on Monday morning we therefore set out for Rheims, on our way to another camp at Charleville. To see the great German Army disorganised, leaderless and in full retreat was a fantastic sight. Trucks, armoured vehicles, tankers, cars running on flattened springs, horse-drawn carts, motor-cycle combinations, even cycles, formed an endless stream going east. Every vehicle carried a watcher on the look-out for Allied aircraft. As soon as one was sighted, the vehicles drew up to the side of the road and the occupants scattered in the surrounding fields. Every hundred yards or so lay a bullet-riddled, burnt-out car or lorry or a smoking tanker. Bodies lay where they had fallen by the roadside, ignored by their living comrades scurrying home to safety.

We reached Rheims at about eleven o'clock, and Cristopher went at once to call on a friend who was in the champagne business. He returned at lunch-time with two cases of Cordon Rouge. Before we could continue our journey, however, it was apparently necessary to get more papers; so Cristopher set out in search of some official who would be able to provide them. While he was away, I sat in the car with a Colonel Bernau, whom we had picked up *en route*. We watched German tanks rumbling eastward in an endless stream, piled high with cases of champagne. When Bernau saw the first of them thus laden, he turned to me and said sadly, 'This is very shameful.' At five o'clock Cristopher returned, and we joined the stream once more. At seven o'clock, as I have since learnt, American tanks entered the city.

We arrived at Charleville about eight o'clock, and spent the night in a disused brothel, which supported a peculiarly vicious type of flea. In the morning Cristopher went to see the Stalag Commandant, who had just given orders to pack up, in readiness to leave in the afternoon for a destination as yet unknown. From him Cristopher managed to obtain some odds and ends of British uniform for me.

We wandered about the town until lunch-time, and I watched a party of German sappers mining the main bridge over the river. At four o'clock we joined the Stalag Staff convoy. While we were waiting to start, Bernau scrounged two dozen tins of Canadian salmon, which, as rations were becoming increasingly difficult to get hold of, were very welcome.

At Sedan there was a halt. After a short wait, the Stalag Commandant told Cristopher that their orders were to go east. Cristopher felt that this would be unwise for us, since he wanted me to be caught up in one of the prison camps before they all moved back into Germany. Hearing that there might still be a camp in the south, we turned towards Montmèdy, near the Franco-Belgian frontier. As dusk began to close in, we pulled up at a farm and commandeered a hay-loft. By wheedling and heavy bribing, we persuaded the farmer's wife to roast a duck and some vegetables for us, which we washed down with a bottle of our Cordon Rouge.

The next day, near Arlon in Belgium, we fell in with another detachment of fugitive S.S. from Paris. They were drawn up in camouflaged positions in a field, waiting for their chief, who had gone to Nancy to try to discover what they were expected to do. Cristopher decided we should wait with them to hear what instructions their chief had been given.

Bernau and I spent the day looking for food, and returned in the late afternoon with a live goose apiece. These we killed, plucked and drew, and then cooked over an open fire for supper. The S.S. chief had still not returned by eight o'clock, so we bedded down in our hay-loft for another night.

Next morning we went back to the field, but as the chief had still not returned, Cristopher decided he would go to Arlon to find out what was happening. Soon after he had left, the chief arrived with orders to move to Strasbourg, and the convoy set off with all speed. Bernau decided that our best plan would be to go towards Arlon, but half-way there we met Cristopher coming back. He had discovered that a little further north, at a place which I cannot now remember, there was an Oflag which had not yet moved. So after some discussion we turned back to Montmèdy; but there we were told that the Americans were in Sedan, and once more turning about, we raced for Arlon, where we arrived at about eight o'clock. Here Cristopher, who had been ill for some days with an intestinal infection, collapsed. Next morning he was still too ill to go on, so we decided to stay until the following day.

On his first trip to Arlon Cristopher had met a party of soldiers with a lorry-load of cigarettes, but no food. He had struck a bargain with them, and had exchanged six of our tins of salmon, which were stored in the back of the car, for ten thousand cigarettes, which he now divided between us.

At the Hotel de la Gare in Arlon I was impressed by the off-hand, almost insolent manner in which the *patron*, his wife and all the staff treated us. These Belgians, who had never been easy under the German yoke, were now only awaiting liberation and were no longer afraid to let the Germans see what they thought of them. Being certain that I had nothing to fear, I sat up for a long while bringing my Paris report up to date and saying exactly what I intended to do. When I had finished it, I put it into an envelope, on which I wrote in French: 'Please hand to the first British or American officer who arrives here, and help England and Belgium.' When we left the hotel next morning, I left the envelope in my room with a hundred cigarettes.

Cristopher was no better, but he insisted on our continuing the journey; so, after passing through Luxembourg, we arrived at Trier, where we were told that the Führer was conferring with Field Marshal von Model.

After lunch, we turned into the lovely Moselle valley. Progress was slow, for the narrow road, crossing and recrossing the river, acted as a bottleneck to the continuous stream of traffic. Wearier soldiers have never taken part in any retreat, famous or infamous. They had been on the go for days, without rest, without orders and without leadership, just going back and back all the time. Retreating from France, they had seized every vehicle they could lay hands on. The magnificent Bugatti in which we had travelled to Vittel was almost new, but had been commandeered without hope of return or redress. As we pushed slowly on up the valley, we passed a convoy of more than a hundred and fifty Paris buses, laden with men, equipment and loot.

In the late afternoon we arrived at Bernkastel on the Moselle. Cristopher's condition had deteriorated so much that we were forced to stop once more. We were all completely exhausted and very glad of the respite. Cristopher and Bernau slept nearly the whole of Sunday, but Cristopher's worries would not let him rest. Although he should have stayed in bed, I could not persuade him to do so, and as we strolled through the village in the cool of the Sabbath dusk, I have never seen a man so bowed with shame.

On Monday we pressed on again, and by lunch-time reached Coblenz, still lovely and undamaged. At four o'clock we came to Limburg, from which Stalag XIIA was only a short distance away.

CHAPTER 16

OFLAG 79

CRISTOPHER and I put up at the Frankfurterhof and Bernau in billets at a private house. On Tuesday Cristopher went out to the Stalag, and also to the transit camp for officers attached to Major-General Fortune's Oflag in Hadamar Schloss. Here he made arrangements for me to become a 'prisoner of war' two days later.

The next day, Cristopher being confined to bed, we made a thorough and final check of the cover stories, S.D. requirements, methods of contact, and all the other things which had to be considered. Since crossing the frontier I had put aside all thoughts of escape; but now the idea of getting myself home to England began to suggest itself again. Apart from personal reasons, which admittedly were strong, I knew that the information I had collected regarding codes, contacts, the operations of the German Intelligence and so on, of which it had been impossible for me to give full details in the report I had left at Arlon, would still be very valuable. I was also troubled by the possibility that in spite of my precautions for its safety, this report might never reach its destination, and the more I thought about it, the more necessary it seemed to me to try to get home. I had been pondering for several days on the method by which I should be most likely to achieve this end, and had reached the conclusion that my best chance of success would be to make a point-blank proposition to Cristopher, accompanied by a false 'confession' of my identity. So after dinner on Wednesday evening I took the plunge.

'Cristopher,' I said, 'I have a confession to make. But before I begin, I want you to be convinced that the story in my dossier, from the moment of my landing at Kiiu Aabla, is the truth. But there is one point which I have concealed. I have made up my mind during the last few days to tell you this, not only because I've grown to like you very much and am grateful to you, but because I trust you as one gentleman naturally trusts another.'

To English ears this speech will certainly sound sentimental and dramatic; but that was what I intended. I had considered it very carefully, and I knew it was just the sort of thing Cristopher would appreciate.

'The point is this,' I went on: 'I am not simply an ordinary agent, which is what I have wanted your Intelligence people to believe. I have the rank of Group-Captain and I am an expert codeographer. My mission to Estonia came about because I was one of the very few Englishmen who speak Estonian and had the necessary knowledge to carry out the job. You yourself come of an old aristocratic family, and will understand what family pride really means. My family has a pretty good record one way and another, and much as I disliked the job, I felt that I had to accept it for the sake of my family's honour. Incidentally just before I left, the King conferred a knighthood on me for my work on codes.

'As you know, I have quite a lot of high political contacts in England, and I am a friend of the Duke of Windsor. I believe that the only hope of preventing Western civilisation from being overrun by Bolshevist barbarity is a firm friendship and understanding between the younger generations of Britain, Germany, and possibly America. The work I'm going to undertake for you is a first step towards this. So let us understand that I am no longer fighting for my life – I am doing this of my own free will.

'But I've been thinking during the last few days that any information I can get for you in these camps is only going to be second-hand. It may well be out of date and is certainly liable to be fairly highly coloured. Now, if I were to return to England, I could re-establish contact with my political friends – Churchill, Bevin, Eden, and the rest – and I would be able to send you absolutely first-hand information, and send it pretty quickly.

'My best friend is the chief liaison officer at the Ministry of Information between the B.B.C., the Government departments and the War Cabinet. [A post which, so far as I know, never existed.] There is no man better placed to have a comprehensive view and knowledge of internal politics at home, as well as in America and the Dominions. We trust each other completely, he and I, and we have often discussed events as they came his way. Now, I could let you have all the information I get rapidly by radio. It would be authentic and up-to-date. I hope,' I concluded, 'that you know me well enough by this time to know that I should never betray your trust.'

As I expected, Cristopher seemed much surprised by all this. Nevertheless, outlandish as some of it may have seemed, I had taken very great care to make it sound as convincing as possible; besides I knew the suggestion held too many possible advantages for him to dismiss it out of hand. We talked it over until the early hours of the morning, and by the time I went to bed he had completely accepted the story and we had agreed on a course of action. It was too late now to cancel the arrangement to get me into the Oflag, for if the Gestapo got to hear of this, which they might easily do through their network of agents, I might still find myself back in Frankfurt gaol. We therefore arranged that for the time being I should carry on with the plan we had worked out at Vittel, so that Cristopher would have something concrete to show his chief when it came to discussing this latest idea with him. Once again I was faced with the situation that the people who knew me and had confidence in me were not those in whose hands lay the final decision about my future.

Having insinuated me into the Oflag, the problem was going to be how to get me out again and back to England. There seemed to be two possible alternatives: either I could 'escape' while being moved to another part of Germany, and make my way to Switzerland; or I could go before a repatriation board. We finally decided that the latter would be the better method, for once I had been interviewed by the board, Cristopher would be able to ensure that its findings would indicate the need for me to be repatriated. After much deliberation, we agreed that the best way for me to get before a board would be to feign gradual insanity. But to convince the board that I was mad meant that I would have to give the same impression to everyone else, for if I were to take the British camp doctors into my confidence, I might easily compromise them. Even if I confided only in the senior officers at the camp, there would still be a risk of the truth about myself leaking out.

Cristopher wisely decided that the fewer people who knew what my real rôle was, the better would be my chance of success, and the better it would be for security. Obviously, the camp commandants would have to be in the picture; so would the Abwehr Security Officer, who would arrange the necessary contacts to collect my reports and send them to S.S. Headquarters in Berlin.

I was the only British officer at Limburg on that Thursday afternoon – the rest were all Americans – when Bernau handed me over to the camp authorities. He told his story convincingly – that he had picked me up in Coblenz, with instructions for me to be sent to the nearest camp. I stayed at Stalag XIIA until Monday, September 10th and on that afternoon, I was taken to the *Kommandantur*, where I found four British officers lying on the grass outside. Shortly afterwards we were taken by train to Hadamar, about six miles away.

I had now assumed the identity of Captain John de Witt, and henceforth was referred to as John D, since it was customary to use Christian names in the camp. That afternoon there were seventy or eighty officers already at the Dulag, waiting for others to arrive. Not until a sufficient number had been collected would the party be transferred to a permanent Oflag. The senior British officer was a Major Peel, to whom, with a committee of majors and a captain or two, I told my story, as arranged with Cristopher.

A day or two later I made my first report and left it under my pillow, where I was to leave them on Monday and Friday mornings, when everyone went out on morning roll-call. It was collected by an Abwehr N.C.O. while the building was empty. To give an idea of the form of the reports and the type of information they contained, this is the sort of thing I wrote:

I was present on Friday at an informal discussion between the following officers, who expressed these views:

Major T. Smith, Royal Tank Corps, age 32, accountant; educated at Oundle and Cambridge, of good family; intelligent and politically aware.

Lt. D. Jones, R.A., age 27, schoolmaster; educated at a good secondary school and teachers' training college; intelligent and obviously thinks.

Capt. H. Robinson, Queen's, age 30, regular soldier; educated at Harrow and Sandhurst, very good family; above average intelligence for a regular officer.

Smith remarked that he thought we were being too trusting in our relations with the Russians. The ultimate objective of Bolshevism had always been world communism, and he did not believe it possible that a nation with such an ideology could suddenly drop it. This war had brought Russia to the forefront of world affairs, and her military successes, based on a very powerful war machine, had placed her in a very strong position in Eastern Europe.

Jones said he believed that as long as we had a

255

strong Conservative government with Churchill or Eden at its head, we should be safe enough. The danger would be if we got a Socialist government. The latter would be so preoccupied with the introduction of new methods of government and working reforms that they would neglect foreign affairs. *Smith* agreed. He held that the Labour Party was insufficiently experienced in government, and further, that the Party had no statesman sufficiently wily to deal successfully with the special type of peasant wiliness which the Russians possessed. The Conservatives had another strong point in their favour; namely, their long experience in government and the tradition of statesmanship and diplomacy handed down in families.

Robinson objected. He pointed out that the leader of the Labour Party had gained valuable experience in the Coalition Government; that men like Attlee and Cripps could very well match the wiliness of the Russians. He maintained that the possibility of peace being preserved would be far greater if a party with a political ideology more akin to the Russians were in power, since it would be able to understand the Russian point of view better and would create greater confidence in the Russians than a Right wing party would be able to create.

Smith said no matter which party got in, he believed a war with Russia to be absolutely unavoidable, if we were to maintain our position as a great world power.

Robinson said the sooner we realised we had already become a second-class power, and devoted all our strength to prevent ourselves from deteriorating into a third-class power, the better. The day of the British Empire and Britain's world domination was over. But we could still have a place among the leading European nations if we tried.

I adhered to my plan of giving, if not exactly opposite views to those that were expressed, at least very distorted ones, and mixing information which I knew the Germans would like to hear with a good measure of what was less palatable, though obviously true.

At the end of ten days I began to lay the foundations of my 'insanity'. From now on, every move I made, every word I spoke, was deliberately planned. Taking into my confidence a number of carefully chosen officers living in my room, I gave it out surreptitiously that I possessed a fortune of a million and a quarter pounds, bequeathed to me by an uncle in Australia. When the war was over I intended using this money to found a train of shops covering the British Isles, which would sell one article only – a meat-filled doughnut, which the Estonians call *pirog*. The profits I made out of this would be devoted to a charity in which I was deeply interested.

I had previously worked out, so I said, an elaborate organisation, and had carefully estimated costs, salaries and so on, which I now submitted to my camp friends. I offered them jobs if they would care to come in with me and help to get the organisation going. Under other circumstances I am sure none of them would have believed a word of all this; but they were bored by the inactivity and confinement, and whether they really believed me or not, they accepted the plan enthusiastically and we all worked together on it for weeks.

Soon after the British attack on Arnhem an influx of new prisoners brought our numbers up to the total required for us to be sent to a permanent Oflag, and on October 22nd we were loaded into cattle trucks and began a journey of two hundred miles from Hadamar to Brunswick, which lasted for five days. It was not very comfortable for me, as I was having another attack of scabies.

Oflag 79 had formerly been the barracks of a Luftwaffe aerodrome, and consisted of seven very large two-storied buildings with cellars and attics, accommodating some two thousand British and Dominion officers and two hundred other ranks. I was posted to Company 9, the Headquarters company. Here we were more fortunate than those in other companies, for our rooms were small, and whereas the average number of men was eighteen to a room, our average was six. Company 9 was also exempted from camp fatigues, as it included a large number of protected personnel. The Senior British Officer (S.B.O.) was Colonel Douglas Brown, who had been captured at Leros.

Spy fever was widespread, and on the arrival of a batch of new prisoners a form of vetting was carried out by the British internal security organisation, familiarly known as 'Cloak and Dagger', or 'C and D.' The Hadamar S.B.O., who had been transferred to Oflag 79 with the rest of us, had told 'C and D' about me as soon as we arrived. When the Camp Security Officer called me in, I told him I would prefer to speak directly to the S.B.O. When I saw him, I told the same story that I had related at Hadamar, including my being a Group Captain and a K.C.B.

Since arriving at Hadamar I had written to my wife, incorporating in code brief notes about what I was doing; for I still had no idea whether my reports from Paris and Arlon had reached their destinations.

Colonel Brown informed me that he had made a rule that no messages might be sent out of the Camp in code without his first censoring them. I had already told him, which I now began to regret, that I had been using a code when communicating with my wife. 'C and D' also had a set of rules, he said, which forbade any man to organise escape on his own initiative. All plans for escape must be submitted to British Security, who would either pass or veto them.

As a result of my experience as an Intelligence Officer in Bomber Command, I knew that in every p.o.w. camp there was at least one officer in possession of a code which enables him to have contact with the War Office. I knew, therefore, that the S.B.O. could – and would – check up on my story. But I also felt pretty sure that the War Office would contact S.O.E., under whose auspices I had received my original training and instructions, and on whose support I knew I could count. However, I had been in captivity more than two years, during which time, unless my reports from Paris and Arlon had got home, no word had been heard from me. So it was perhaps not altogether surprising that the War Office's message in answer to Colonel Brown's enquiry was, as I learnt much later: 'Treat with the gravest suspicion.'

Ten days after my arrival at Oflag 79, I was taken with a party of officers, to the *Kommandantur* to be questioned by the Abwehr officers. There I found Cristopher, who introduced me to the German Camp Welfare Officer, Dr Ackermann, and together we devised a scheme for me to hand over my reports.

I was to accost Dr Ackermann one morning in the

compound, and ask him to obtain some piano music for me. Ten days later Ackermann was to send for me to come to the *Kommandantur*, on the pretext of my consulting a catalogue. We were to make contact subsequently in the same way, using musical excuses. This was necessary because another of Colonel Brown's rules was that whenever an officer was summoned to the *Kommandantur*, immediately he returned within the wire he must report to the Adjutant on what had happened.

We believed that the musical excuse could function until Christmas without arousing the suspicions of 'C and D', but another method would have to be devised for the New Year. I did not like Cristopher's references to the New Year, because I was sure that the S.D. would become aware of my deception by Christmas – and I wanted to get home. Even now, to allay suspicion, we arranged for Lieutenant Habehauer, the Abwehr Officer, to send for me once or twice about alleged discrepancies in registration cards. As a matter of fact, I had been twice registered as a p.o.w. – once at Limburg and again at Hadamar. The story I told 'C and D' was that the registration at Limburg had been done in a hurry by American interpreters. The two cards had now arrived at Oflag 79 and the particulars on the cards did not tally. It was obviously a case of carelessness by the American who had filled in the Limburg card, for under my name were the particulars of some other man.

At this first meeting with Cristopher in Oflag 79 he told me he had received provisional approval from Berlin for the plan to send me back to England; so now it was up to me to bring myself before a repatriation board.

I therefore renewed work on my mammoth business project, and also made promises of financial help to several officers. At the same time I began to spread stories of persecution by senior officers and the S.B.O., using as my agents some of the padres, in whom I knew the propensity for parochial gossip to be well-developed. I also dropped hints about an extensive and beautiful country property in England and of other valuable possessions. I talked of my intimacy with the Duke of Windsor and the Royal family, and claimed to be a particular protégé of the Prime Minister, to whom I said I was directly responsible.

Finally, I began to talk to a chosen few about a German Foreign Office official whom I had met on my way from Germany to France, who had asked me whether I would be prepared to carry back to England proposals for another *coup d'état* by an anti-Nazi faction. As a result of this, I said, I expected to be taken out of the camp at any moment. I now began also to hoard food and act oddly in other ways.

Since leaving Paris I had had Thérèse Lupin very much on my conscience, and had written to her from Hadamar to try to find out what had happened to her. Having received no reply, I wrote again on November 1st, putting after my signature the monogram on my signet-ring, which we had adopted as a private security check during the hectic last days in Paris. In the camp there was a voluntary censorship of all outgoing mail, which was carried out by three lieutenant-colonels, and on November 7th I was summoned by Colonel Brown, who produced my letter from his tray, saying, as he did so:

'My Security Officer suspects that there is a code message in this letter. You know what my regulations are.'

I told him the letter contained no such message, and that in any case I had promised not to send any messages without showing them to him first. I also pointed out that I had posted the letter in Company 9's letter-box seven days ago, and protested against my mail being held up for so long, when it already took a considerable time for letters to reach their destination. When the interview came to an end we were both rather heated.

At the beginning of December, Dr Ackermann told me that Cristopher would be arriving in the first week of the New Year for a long discussion. The problem was how we were to meet. Eventually I suggested that I should be arrested by Habehauer, the Abwehr officer, on the grounds that Berlin's suspicions had been excited by my two registration cards; orders had been received that my belongings were to be searched and that I was to be taken to the *Kommandantur* for interrogation, and kept in the cells there. To this plan Dr Ackermann agreed.

In the middle of December it became obvious inside the wire that a certain piece of information had reached the Germans, indicating that there was a dangerous leakage from inside the camp. Shortly after this, while I was on one of my periodic visits to Dr Ackermann, he referred to this piece of information. Taken off my guard, I expressed some surprise that the *Kommandantur* should be aware of it; to which the Doctor replied, 'You are not our only contact in the camp, you know.'

This knowledge placed me in a quandary. I could not go to the S.B.O. and tell him what I knew, since it would have meant revealing my real activities. Yet if the informer were allowed to go on giving information, the lives of many prisoners in the camp might be endangered. I decided, therefore, that I must somehow draw attention to this leakage in such a way as to make it unsafe for the informer to continue. I therefore tried to arrange that someone should see me talking to Ackermann, but that they should be too far off to be able to identify me.

As I slept badly, it was my custom to get up early every morning and go to Holy Communion in the chapel, which was in one of the cellars. I told Ackermann that those in the orderly room were becoming suspicious of my constant visits to the *Kommandantur*, and suggested that in future we should meet near the chapel at this hour when there was usually no one else about.

At our first meeting, which was on December 19th, our company Adjutant, who enjoyed a solitary tramp round the compound between half-past six and half-past seven, was the only person we saw. But on December 29th when we met for the second time, we were seen by others. I learned later that while all this was taking place, the message arrived from the War Office to treat me with the gravest suspicion!

'C and D' were soon hot on the trail. They set all sorts of traps for me, into some of which I walked deliberately; the rest I avoided.

One of these traps involved our secret radio, which provided the B.B.C. news bulletins. The Germans were aware of its existence, and did their best to locate the set, but without success. Very few of the prisoners knew where it was hidden and during each broadcast an elaborate system of scouts kept watch. These scouts were taken from the Camp fatigue company of the week, and were very carefully picked. Headquarters company, as I have already mentioned, were exempt from camp fatigues. Yet now, for some apparently inexplicable reason, the company was suddenly given a week's duty.

When the company Security Officer's representative

came round with the radio scout rota, the five other officers in my room were allotted times, but I was left out.
When I did not rise to the bait and ask my room companions where they went, or even attempt to follow them,
my room commander provoked a discussion in which he
remarked casually, as though assuming my attention to be
elsewhere, 'The radio is in the attic of House 7.'

It was assumed, I suppose, that as soon as I told the
Germans this, they would search House 7 – by which
time, of course, the radio would have been moved to
another spot – and thus it would be known that I had
given the information. If only the S.B.O. and the rest had
known exactly what the B.B.C. bulletins meant to me!
The months were rushing by, and the front ran from
Antwerp to the Rhine. If my plan for getting home did
not succeed soon, the false information I was passing to
Cristopher would be discovered for what it was, and that
would be the end of everything.

On January 2nd, I was to meet Ackermann in the
compound, ostensibly to return some music to him, while
he was to tell me the date of Cristopher's arrival.
Ackermann was delayed, and when he did arrive at the
rendezvous I was not there. Rather foolishly, the good
Doctor paced up and down not far from the Orderly
Room, obviously waiting for someone. He was observed;
and so was I, when I eventually found him and hurried

to my room to get the music. It was also noticed that we had a short conversation; during it he told me that Cristopher was arriving on January 4th and that Lieutenant Habehauer would come to my room and arrest me at half-past three that afternoon.

Two days later I was sitting over a mug of tea with the others, when Habehauer and two soldiers threw open the door and strode in. He searched me and my bed and locker, confiscated the manuscript of a play I was writing, then informed me that I was under arrest and escorted me to the *Kommandantur*.

CHAPTER 17

PROTECTIVE CUSTODY

AT midnight Cristopher came to see me in the detention cell at the *Kommandantur*, bringing with him a bottle of wine, and we talked until nearly four in the morning. He told me that my reports were eagerly awaited in Berlin, and that through them I had gained the confidence of the highest authorities, who had given permission for our plan to proceed at once. He now wished me to intensify my efforts, so that I might be brought before a repatriation board which was due to sit in February.

Before I returned to the camp on the Saturday morning, I again saw Ackermann. He told me that the S.B.O. had protested vehemently about my arrest, and had been informed that I had been interrogated on instructions from Berlin, and that as I had refused to answer some of the questions, I had been put in the cells to have an opportunity of changing my mind.

I returned to the compound to find that no one had expected to see me again, and that there had, in fact, been several applicants for my bed. When I had eaten, I went to the S.B.O.'s office to give an account of my experiences.

I told the S.B.O. that when I had arrived at the *Kommandantur* on Thursday, Habehauer had said that he had received orders from Berlin to question me about my antecedents. I had told him that I had nothing to add to what I had already told him. Habehauer replied that in that case he would give me an opportunity to think it over. On Friday I had been twice interrogated and had made a statement repeating my original story.

Colonel Brown replied that he was very worried for my safety. He knew for certain that there had been a leakage of information, and in his opinion I had been rather indiscreet.

I felt quite certain that he was planning some move against me. I could sense it, not only during my meetings with him, and with the Security Officer, but from the atmosphere of my room, and I now began to wonder what form his action would take. I was terribly afraid that my plans might be jeopardised by 'C and D', though I appreciated that they were only trying to protect themselves.

Early in December, before all this had started, my room commander, Major Law, who was a motor-racing enthusiast, had been discussing cars with me and I had offered to lend him some money with which to buy a car after the war. I had suggested a loan of a thousand pounds at one per cent interest, the capital to be repaid in instalments. Not unnaturally, the offer was refused. But I suspected that my purpose in making it, which had been to give Major Law doubts about my sanity, had been achieved.

After supper, before the news reading, a message was read out from the S.B.O. It said: 'I have reason to believe that there is an informer in the camp. Any officer who has anything to say about it should report immediately to his Company Security Officer.'

The next morning, just after chapel, Major Ricky Wall, Company 9's commander, asked me to take a stroll with him. When we were out of earshot he said, 'The S.B.O wants to have another word with you about this affair.'

As we walked over to the Orderly Room he was extremely affable and I was rather at sea, wondering more than ever what their attitude was going to be. They were treating me, I thought, rather like a bad-tempered child who has to be humoured for the sake of peace. I wondered if they imagined that I still did not know what was going on, and were trying to lull me into a false state of security.

We went into the Orderly Room, and the Adjutant announced us to the S.B.O., taking up his stand on the other side of me from Wall, as if I were a prisoner on a charge.

'I am very worried about you, de Witt,' Colonel Brown began. 'Since my notice yesterday evening I have had a constant stream of officers coming to see me with the most fantastic stories about you. I know you will be the first to agree that your own account of your activities up to now is very queer. It appears, however, that you've been broadcasting it to all and sundry; very stupidly, if I may say so.

'The padres have reported several curious things, and now Major Law tells me that last night, after you heard my notice, you made him an offer of a thousand pounds.'

The implication of the last sentence was too much.

'Ask him to think again,' I broke in. 'Perhaps he will remember that I gave it to him *before* the news. Why I offered it to him is a private matter between him and me.'

'That's as may be,' Brown answered, 'but let me go on. From several people comes a strange story about a vast business you are planning.'

It appeared that practically everybody to whom I had spoken had gone running to report what I had said, whether it had any bearing on the situation or not. But I still did not know what line Colonel Brown had decided to take.

'You have been down to the *Kommandantur* many times,' he went on, 'to see Dr Ackermann. The other day he was seen looking about the compound for you, quite distracted, and you dashed up to him and handed him some documents. I don't know whether you understand the serious

271

position you are in. Many officers believe you to be an informer, and if they should choose to take the law into their own hands, I could not guarantee to be answerable for your safety.' He had been watching me closely as he spoke, almost as though he had been expecting violence. 'I have talked to the doctors about you,' he went on, 'and they have told me that they consider you to be mentally ill. So I have decided that you must be protected from yourself.'

I dared not let him see what an immense relief it was to hear those words.

'And do *you* think I am mad?' I asked, trying to sound both plaintive and incredulous at the same time.

The Colonel shrugged politely. 'For your own sake I've decided to place you in protective custody. You will not be allowed to leave your room unless accompanied by an officer. It will not be pleasant for you, but you will have to put up with it.'

The S.B.O. was quite right – it would not be very pleasant; but it might be much worse.

He stood up, and we rose too.

'I hope,' I said, 'that I shall have an opportunity of proving to you that I am not mad.'

'I'm sure you will,' the Colonel answered; but he did not sound convinced.

I could scarcely believe that I had carried my plan so

far with success, and that the doctors were really convinced that I was mentally unbalanced. Even so, I still had to persuade them that I was so far gone that they would have to arrange for my repatriation.

My room companions behaved as gentlemen do in unpleasant and uncomfortable circumstances. A few friends went out of their way to show me that although they dared not say so openly, they still trusted me; consequently I felt more despicable than ever.

The idea of putting me under protective custody had, of course, only one object: if I were really an informer the Germans would prove it by trying to get me out of the camp as soon as they heard of it, unless I were to betray myself beforehand by trying to get in touch with them. I fully appreciated that Colonel Brown was bound to act as he had, otherwise he would have failed in his duty; for on him rested the responsibility for the safety of some two thousand British officers in the camp.

Less than a week after the axe had fallen on me, the following message was circulated:

Lt —, who has recently been removed from the camp by the Germans under suspicious circumstances, must be considered to have been an informer.

On January 16th I was awakened by the Company Adjutant and instructed to report at the main gate of the compound at eight o'clock to go to Brunswick Hospital for a medical examination. I got up, ate some biscuit porridge, and then walked the five miles into Brunswick, accompanied by a single guard.

At the Inselwald Hospital we stood in a queue for an hour, and as we were about to go in to the doctor, an air-raid alarm sounded. For more than two hours we remained in a large surface shelter, and when we returned to the hospital, the doctor we were to see had left, leaving instructions that we were to come again on January 18th.

On Thursday I was again taken to the hospital. The guard handed the doctor a paper, which he read, then turned to me and asked: 'Do you speak German?'

'No,' I said.

'French?'

'Yes, I speak French.'

'Voulez-vous traduire cette note, s'il vous plaît?'

I took the paper and translated into French:

This officer came to this camp in October last in a very nervous condition and suffering from scabies. Recently he has become worse. He suffers from delusions of persecution, makes himself out to have been knighted, has made a brother officer an offer of £1,000 and offered jobs to several officers in a business scheme involving some £500,000.

I believe him to be suffering from paranoic schizo-phrenia.

(Signed)———.

Lt.-Col., R.A.M.C.

Senior British Medical Officer.

I stripped and was given a thorough examination. While I was dressing, the doctor dictated a report in German to his secretary. He said that he could not pass an opinion on a cursory examination and recommended that I should be sent elsewhere for observation. This was not at all what I wanted, for it might mean a serious interruption of my plans.

On our return to the Oflag, I went to the *Kommandantur* and insisted on seeing Dr Ackermann, to whom I recounted all that had happened.

'We know,' replied the Doctor, 'and the Commandant is furious; you have frightened the other man, and he refuses to help us any more.'

I begged Ackermann to get in touch urgently with Cristopher and ask him to set things in motion from his end as quickly as possible.

The weeks that followed were terrible, and to the strain of waiting was added the failure of our Red Cross food parcels — cigarettes had run out before Christmas — and as at the same time the Germans cut the rations they allowed us, there was scarcely any food. Nerves, tempers and morale deteriorated. The S.B.O. was compelled to visit the companies and give pep-talks, and a German Foreign Office official, Colonel Hertzog, arrived, but could do nothing to help us; the German Commandant, Colonel Strehle, was replaced. Then came the news that the Russians had broken through to within thirty miles of Berlin.

When Cristopher gave no sign, I began to fear that Berlin was being evacuated and that he had had no time to attend to me. For the third time I was going to fail within sight of my goal.

On February 2nd I was instructed to report again to the hospital; so I went, wondering whether I should return to the Oflag, or whether the British had unwittingly forestalled Cristopher. In Brunswick, however, Dr Ackermann met me, and told me that Cristopher was coming for me soon. There had been another change in our plans. The repatriation scheme was off and an alternative plan for my escape was to be carried out. I told him that if Cristopher did not come soon I really should go mad; and indeed, in the days that followed I often felt it was touch and go whether I should remain sane. But another five weeks went by before I heard from Cristopher.

On Sunday, March 11th, I was lying on my bed after lunch, when the British Assistant Camp Adjutant put his head round the door and said that I was wanted immediately at the *Kommandantur*. I dressed and went alone through the deserted camp – few officers in these days had the strength to walk about much – and in the Security Office at the *Kommandantur* I found Cristopher. He indicated a man in civilian clothes, and two others in S.S. uniform.

'This gentleman,' he said, 'is from the local Gestapo, and these two officers from the S.S. have come to take you away. We have sent for the S.M.O. and he will be questioned about the report he made to the German doctor. It will be made clear to him that this report has aroused the suspicions of the Berlin authorities, and we have found out that you are a dangerous British agent, Ronald Seth, who escaped from the prison in Frankfurt in 1944.'

The S.M.O. was brought into an adjoining office. I was marched through, casting at him what I hoped was an injured and disillusioned look. In the corridor I turned and came into a room on the other side of the Security Office; there, standing behind the door, I listened to the S.M.O. being questioned. I really felt sorry for him; though I am sure he tried hard, he did not sound very convincing as he protested that he knew me only as Captain de Witt;

that he really believed me to be insane, and had wanted to bring me before a repatriation board only in order to help me. It was definitely not because he knew that I was a British agent that he had wished to do so. He had not the slightest idea of this.

CHAPTER 18

BERLIN

I

WHEN he had gone, I was marched by the S.S. officers to a waiting car and driven to a hotel in Brunswick, where Cristopher had already reserved a room. He had brought civilian clothes for me, and for once I was happy to get out of the remnants of my uniform.

During dinner he told me that the Regional Security Officer would like to ask me a few questions, and that he would be joining us shortly.

'But it's up to you,' Cristopher said. 'As I promised from the beginning, I've never asked you to give us military information. I don't know what the R.S.O. wants, and if you'd rather not see him you needn't. But he did help us to arrange this afternoon's little comedy; so, if you would agree to see him, I should be very grateful. You can hear his questions first, and if they embarrass you, don't answer.'

I said I could see no harm in discovering what the officer wanted. Privately I thought that his questions might reveal some information; so when he arrived I was there to meet him. He spoke in laboured English.

'Sir,' he began, 'I have here a document which gives certain particulars of what is happening within Oflag 79. We have verified much of it, but there are one or two points on which we should like to have confirmation.'

I took the typewritten translation which he held out to me, and read it through. It gave a full description of the S.B.O's secret organisation of the camp into battalions, with the names of the commanders, and the tasks allotted to each, should active resistance be necessary towards the end. It also gave the names of the British Camp Security Officer and his assistants, and described how the secret radio set was camouflaged inside a gramophone. It stated that there was a camera in the camp, and that photographs had been taken of all the German officers for a future black list. It even described where the negatives were hidden and gave one of the German guards as the source of supply of the films.

These were the chief points, and it was quite obvious from the manner in which the R.S.O. accepted my replies that he believed me when I said that I had never heard the Security Officer's name, that I knew nothing of the location of the radio set, since I had taken special pains to remain in ignorance of it; that I knew there was some organisation for an emergency, but had never bothered to find out about it, because I had not thought that I should be in the camp when the end came; and that I thought the hidden negatives sounded like a flight of fancy.

When he departed shortly afterwards, Cristopher and I went up to bed. Lying on springs for the first time for months, smoking a cigarette, and with a glass of cognac beside me, I listened while Cristopher outlined the new plan. He explained that they had a very important task for me to undertake. He could not say what it was; that was to be left to someone higher up. In connection with it, however, he had been appointed Vice-Consul in Zurich, and would be setting out for Switzerland with his family at the end of the week. My task would not take long to accomplish, and when it had been done, the plan under which I was to provide political information would be carried out.

'You believe then,' I said, 'that Germany can still hold on?'

'No one can say anything with any degree of certainty,' he answered, 'but in the highest quarters it is believed that circumstances will arise in which your work will be very useful.'

With that I had to be content.

The next morning, March 11th, we took the train to Berlin. In these days the Berliner going out shopping never knew whether his home would still be standing when he returned. So every time he went more than a few hundred yards from home, he carried all that was left of his wardrobe in a suitcase. Cristopher, too, had all his belongings in a suitcase and a rucksack, and as we neared his

281

flat, we saw that though the house was undamaged, the one next door had been razed by a direct hit. The flat had been partly dismantled when he had moved his family to the Rhineland, but we made ourselves as comfortable as we could.

During the next few weeks I did all the shopping and cooking and kept the place clean, and in between times received instructions for my operation. As I again weighed less than ten stone by this time, the S.S. provided me with three times the rations of an officer on leave. They also gave me identification papers, and once more I became Härra Sven Paasikivi, though this time I was a Swede.

These days of March 1945, in Berlin, when the Americans and British were dashing in from the West, and the Russians were at Kustrin, less than forty miles away, almost defy description. The extent of the damage was bewildering, particularly in the centre of the city and the administrative quarter of the Wilhelmstrasse and the Unter den Linden. There were huge gaps in the buildings, and the streets were piled high with rubble. The Nicholas Cathedral, at the entrance to the Kurfurstendamm, was a shell, and there were great gashes among the blocks of shops, which had been patched up and were open for business, though empty of supplies. Even on the brightest day everyone and everything appeared incredibly dirty. The people lived in the damp, unhealthy cellars of their shattered homes, and no one had more belongings than could be got into a couple of suitcases. Everyone looked shabby, pinched, bad-tempered and proud. Yet they still had faith in the Führer. He would yet do something which would roll up the Russians and smash the Allied Powers. Tired and dirty, and longing for peace though they were, they wanted only peace with victory.

Communications were appalling. The trains were few and crowded and there were no buses. Electricity was cut, except for a few hours a day, and the gas pressure was so low that it was useless. The only fuel available for cooking was the charred wood from bombed houses. Food was scarce, and becoming scarcer every day. A box of matches cost the equivalent of ten shillings – and not on the black market. Bread and potatoes were the staple diet, and there were not many potatoes. I cannot conceive how ordinary civilians, whose rations were less than those of an officer on leave, were able to satisfy their hunger, for even my triple rations were not enough to prevent my feeling hungry.

At nine-thirty every night, so punctually that one might set one's watch by it, the air-raid warning sounded. All the time I was in Berlin the Mosquitoes were establishing their record of forty-seven consecutive nights over the German capital. We would put on all the clothes we could, pick up our suitcases, radio and briefcase, and go down to the cellars – if we were still fortunate enough to be living above ground.

Every shelter had its radio tuned in to raid-information. The loud-speaker would tell us: 'The first wave of ten heavy bombers, accompanied by fighters, is twenty kilometres north-north-west of Magdeburg, flying on an easterly course . . . Single fighter-bombers are approaching Potsdam on a north-westerly course . . . Fighter-bombers are only over the north and south-west suburbs of Berlin . . .'

Going to the entrance of the shelter and looking up at the bright moonlit sky – as brilliant as the moon over Kiiu Aabla in October, 1942 – one could hear the throb of engines; then would come the shrill descending whistle, and as one ducked inside, a far-off crump, or sometimes a nearby roar.

Presently, the radio would tell us: 'The first waves of single fighter-bombers are turning south and leaving Berlin . . . the fifth wave . . . the tenth wave . . . the Berlin region is now free of enemy aircraft.' Then the 'yellow' would sound, and five minutes later the all-clear. But sometimes as we went upstairs, we heard the drone of a single aircraft overhead, and a moment later, as we threw ourselves flat, the whistle of a bomb, then a crump just up the street. Even the German warning system occasionally made mistakes.

Once I was caught in a daylight raid at the Adlon Hotel

and spent several hours, squashed and sweating, among the *élite* of Berlin. Another time I was near the Zoo, and was shepherded into the gigantic surface shelter close by, which accommodated over one hundred thousand people and was equipped with dormitories, canteens and hospitals. Once I was in Schmargandorf, the residential suburb, and watched the sky over the Wilhelmstrasse, dark as night with a heavy pall of smoke.

I saw war-weary Germans refusing to believe they could be defeated while their Führer lived; I saw them rallying to the calls of Goebbels, who bewitched them with his words, and of Bormann, who played upon their good nature and common sense. I saw them panting along the shores of the Halensee with clubs and knives, as I had seen the staff of the B.B.C. Home Guard – then the L.D.V. – doing rifle drill with broomsticks in the Concert Hall at Broadcasting House back in 1940. I saw them queueing for food that they knew they would never get, and searching the ruins of their former homes for small belongings; I saw them consummating their love in shattered doorways and against trees before it was dark enough to hide their quest for something pleasurable, however fleeting; I saw them lavishing parent-love on deformed and sickly children. I looked upon them, these people who dwelt among the ruins of their city, and my heart wept for my enemies.

II

Before Cristopher went off to Zürich we prepared the whole scheme of my operation. My instructions were simple. I was to send back by radio every political event and item of any importance. The S.D. had now sufficient confidence in my political judgment to give me *carte blanche* as regards what to send and what to omit.

My cover story for use at home was, of course, to be the same, up to my leaving Oflag 79. Briefly, I had escaped from Frankfurt Prison, had reached Paris and joined the Maquis; and had been captured while trying to get to the British lines. The camp episode would, of course, explain itself, since nothing could be proved against me, except that I had visited Dr Ackermann perhaps more frequently than was wise.

The comedy played at the *Kommandantur* with the S.M.O. was logical enough. Berlin's suspicions having been roused, and the finger-prints taken at Frankfurt having been found to be identical with those on my registration card, the Gestapo had come to the camp and arrested me. I had been kept for some days in Brunswick Prison, and then taken to the Stalag at Leuchenwalde, a few miles south-west of Berlin, for identification and questioning. Then it had been decided to send me to Dachau concentration camp, just north of Munich.

Thereafter my story was that shortly before reaching

Dachau, the train in which I was being transported was attacked by the R.A.F. As invariably happened, all the passengers scattered, and in the panic I was able to evade my escort. I broke into a house and stole civilian clothes, food and cigarettes, in return for which French workers later gave me more food. Travelling on foot, I by-passed Munich, and then boarding a train, reached Bregenz, on Lake Constance. Once again on foot, I came to the Swiss frontier and during the night got under the wire, and so came back to England.

Again the problem arose of how I should obtain a radio for sending back my messages. I suggested once more that I should make one, but the experts at the Havel Institute – the Secret Service radio headquarters – opposed it, and soon afterwards produced a combined transmitter and receiver, ten inches by three, weighing only two pounds. It was the very latest in secret radio equipment, and I knew that the authorities at home would be delighted to have it. The question then arose of how I was to get it to England, and after much consideration the following plan was decided on. The radio set, with accessories and several other small items, were to be sent to Cristopher in Zürich by the diplomatic bag. He would go to a certain shop in Berne, buy a large box of chocolates and hide the equipment under the first layer. All prisoners of war escaping to Switzerland were taken to the British Legation at Berne, and were allowed complete freedom of movement. So when I arrived there, I was to ask for money for a shopping expedition, and would buy several parcels, which I would ask the shops to deliver at the British Legation. The same day the Germans in Berne would send the box of chocolates containing the radio to me at the Legation. Prisoners of war returning home were given wide latitude both by French and British customs officials, and it was considered that the risks of the radio being discovered were negligible.

I would naturally have to travel down to Munich and along the route I would have taken, had I really escaped, so that my answers to any geographical questions should be correct. When I arrived at Munich a telegram was to be sent to Cristopher at Zürich, saying that his 'motor-car' was waiting in Munich. He would then meet me there and see me over the frontier.

For longer reports, which could not be sent by radio, I was to use the newest thing in secret inks, which was apparently so perfect that no known test could disclose its presence. As the ingredients were in tablet form, a number of the tablets were to be included in the radio parcel. I suggested that to guard against accidents, I should take two tablets with me, since they looked like aspirins and could be swallowed harmlessly, and this was agreed.

A series of advertisements were prepared for me to insert

in certain newspapers, indicating what sort of reception I had received at home, or if I thought I was in imminent danger of arrest, or if, for some reason, I was unable to use my radio.

There was a delay of some days before a wireless instructor could be spared to teach me German radio procedure and codes; but eventually a young Viennese Nazi, as temperamental as a chorus girl and as nervous as a novice, appeared, and we settled down to work. Another civilian gave me instruction in the use of the secret ink.

Several people from S.D. Headquarters, who were involved in arranging the operation, came to see me, regarding me as an object of great curiosity – the one and only agent of the British Secret Service whom most of them had ever seen. Nothing that could be done for my comfort was omitted. I was given five hundred marks for pocket money, and also cigarettes and pipe tobacco, which at that time were unprocurable in Berlin, except among the S.D.

On March 16th Cristopher went to Hamburg to collect his family, who had moved there from the Rhineland, and a young S.S. officer, Lieutenant Willy Tiesler, joined me at the flat.

As I said *au revoir* to Cristopher, who was excited and nervous about getting his family to Switzerland before the

Allies' expected offensive began in the spring, he suddenly blurted out, 'I don't advise you to double-cross us. Don't forget we have plenty of evidence that you have betrayed your country.'

When he saw my look of astonishment, he stopped abruptly and looked confused, as though remembering suddenly that a German gentleman should never forget himself.

'Please forget that, Ronny,' he said uncomfortably. 'You know we have absolute confidence in you. Till Munich, then.'

'Till Munich,' I answered. Despite all his protestations of friendship, I realised now that I had been wise in constantly reminding myself that if I made the slightest slip, he would be among the first to demand my head.

His journey from Hamburg to Zürich took ten days. On Good Friday, March 30th, we heard he had arrived.

CHAPTER 19

HIMMLER'S SPECIAL AGENT

THE day before he had left for Hamburg – March 15th – Cristopher had taken me to the Adlon Hotel, where he introduced me to a friend, whom he called Baron X. The Baron was an Under-Secretary at the Foreign Office, a well known career diplomat, who, having joined the S.D. in 1933, had served as liaison officer between Ribbentrop and Himmler from 1936 to 1939, and in 1938 had been appointed to the post he still held. I was told that Goebbels said of him that he was a mediocre figure, 'at best only a high-grade private secretary,' and that there could be no question whatever of his having any influence on foreign policy. Goebbels may have been right, but the man I now met was doing his best to have a finger in shaping the end of the war.

After introducing us, and arranging to call back for me later on, Cristopher left us together. Over lunch the Baron talked incessantly, beginning with a reiteration of the statements and views of most Germans concerning the war with Great Britain. 'It should never, need never, have been.' The long campaign in Russia had naturally weakened the German forces, and as Russia advanced into eastern Europe, so the threat grew to the foundations of culture and civilisation as the western world knew it. No man who had the welfare of the human race at heart could fail to see where his duty lay. The only way in which this cataclysmic event could be avoided was by a concerted effort of the western people against Russia.

Within the German Foreign Office and the Political Department of the S.D., the Baron continued, there were certain circles who realised this and were prepared to make every sacrifice for its accomplishment. These men knew that there could never be a *rapprochement* between the Western Allies and the present German régime. People like Ribbentrop, Ley and Goebbels would have to go. The political basis of Germany would have to be changed, and they were prepared to do all this.

I had been brought to the notice of this group by Count Dönhoff, and it had been agreed to ask me to act as liaison between them and Mr Churchill. Being personally acquainted with him, I would be able to approach him direct.

'But how am I to explain why I, among the many thousands of prisoners, came to be chosen for this?' I asked.

'We have thought of that,' the Baron answered. 'You may say that we did not wish to approach what we call the *élite* prisoners, such as the King's nephew, because, as soldiers, they would suspect a trick. In any case, I doubt if any of them would accept. Oflag 79 is the largest in

Germany, so it would be natural for us to look there. As you know, one of our representatives, Colonel Hertzog, has recently been there. Let us assume, shall we, that he has talked to you, and recommended you to us? The method by which you were taken out of the camp was organised by us. You were brought secretly to Berlin and helped to escape.'

To me this seemed just another clumsy piece of German security. It would not have stood the test of a really searching interrogation, except, on the Goebbels principle – that it is the incredible which is always likely to happen. Since, however, the Baron seemed satisfied with the story, I was prepared to accept it.

'And what about the story that has been arranged with Count Dönhoff?' I asked.

'The S.D. men who are preparing you for operation 22D [this was the scheme I had arranged with Cristopher] do not, and indeed must not, know of our plan. This is something entirely separate from the arrangements made by Count Dönhoff, and it is vital to keep the matter completely secret. What you have to do is to learn all we tell you, and keep silent. To satisfy your instructors for 22D, however, you must have a cover story, and the Count's will do. But you will not use it, of course, in England.'

At this moment the air-raid sirens sounded, and there began a dignified scramble for the shelters.

'Will you do this?' the Baron asked as we stood up.

'Of course,' I replied; and we too, joined the scramble. This was the occasion on which I sat for nearly three hours squashed by the cream of Berlin society.

After Cristopher went off to Hamburg, I heard nothing more about the proposal for some days. I then received a visit from a Lieut-Colonel Paeffgan, Chief of the S.S. Political Department, and second-in-command to General Schellenberg, one of Himmler's right-hand men. Paeffgan, a tall, blond Swabian, who even in private conversation spoke in the resonant tones of a public orator, was something of a mystery man. He had never come into the Nazi limelight and very little is known about him.

He was accompanied by his Personal Assistant, Captain Pretsch, and to act as interpreter there was Willy Tiesler, the young S.S. lieutenant who had joined me when Cristopher left for Switzerland. At this, and at two or three subsequent interviews, Paeffgan outlined certain proposals that I was to submit privately to Mr Churchill.

On Good Friday, March 30th, Paeffgan, with Baron X as interpreter, went over every minute detail of the proposals and made me learn by heart their exact wording, as I should be unable to take a written document. Great stress was laid on the point that I must insist that Mr Eden should not be present when I saw the Prime Minister, since he was very strongly anti-Nazi, and his influence over Mr Churchill was well known.

After they had gone Willy received instructions that we were to get ready to go to Munich on the night train the following evening. Just before lunch on Saturday, however, these orders were cancelled, and we were told to be ready to leave on Easter Monday.

On Easter Sunday at about half-past nine, Willy received a call from Pretsch asking him to go to S.D. Headquarters to collect some tickets for a concert to which we were both going in the afternoon. While he was away I began preparing lunch, and was scraping a handful of wizened carrots when the doorbell rang. Cursing Willy's absent-mindedness in forgetting his latch-key, which he had often done before, I went to open the door. But instead of Willy I found four men, two of whom were in uniform. The entrance-hall was dark, but I recognised Paeffgan's voice when he asked if I were alone. I said that I was, and they came inside.

In the light of the sitting-room I recognised two of my other visitors: one was Baron X; the other was Chief of the S.S., Heinrich Himmler. The fourth I later discovered was General Schellenberg.

I asked them to sit down and took the cigarette that was offered me. Himmler peered at me through his spectacles and said in German, 'So this is the young man.'

'*Jawohl, Herr Reichsführer*,' boomed Paeffgan.

'His instructions are clear?' Himmler asked the Baron, who turned to me and translated.

'Perfectly,' I replied.

'And he is not afraid that there will be trouble for him in England?'

'None at all,' I said. 'The S.D. have made thorough preparations.'

'He realises that he must, absolutely, make Churchill agree?'

'Certainly.'

'Does he think he will be successful?'

'I have no doubt at all.'

There was a pause. Himmler continued to stare at me.

'He is very young,' he said at last.

'How old are you?' asked the Baron.

'Thirty-three,' I said.

When the Baron translated, Himmler repeated, 'Yes, very young; it is very important work.'

Paeffgan, the Baron and Himmler spoke volubly together in German, and as I listened my heart sank. Here was the old trouble. The highest authority was doubtful. Paeffgan praised my political acumen; the Baron stressed my fitness from the point of view of birth and personal acquaintance with the Prime Minister; but it was the General who apparently settled the matter. 'We know of no one else,' he said, 'and time is short.'

Himmler stood up, and the others also rose. He held out his hand to me, clicked his heels, bowed stiffly, and said, '*Viel Glück!*'

At the door the Baron said, 'You must speak of this visit to no one.'

They had been there less than a quarter of an hour, and I went back to my carrots feeling unutterably depressed. Could it really be possible that for the third time all my planning and suffering had been to no purpose, that the whole scheme was to be stultified at the last moment? However, I was still Agent 22D, of course, as well as Himmler's special agent, so that even if he pronounced his veto, the other arrangements would presumably stand.

The following proposals are those which I had memorised to place before Mr Churchill.

Sure in the conviction that the Prime Minister of England realises the threat to civilisation from the constant advance of the Russian Armies into eastern Europe, some members of the German Foreign Office and of the S.S. make the following observations to the Prime Minister:

It is clear that should the Russian Armies prove victorious, the Russians have every intention of using the military power of Germany to further their aims of world conquest.

The setting up of the Seydlitz Committee in Moscow proves this. Rather than see the eclipse of German arms, it is known that many members of the German Supreme Command would be willing to co-operate with the Russian High Command.

The internal state of Germany has now become so disorganised that the only body capable of maintaining discipline among the civilian population is the S.S. As a result of the Allied bombing more than 30,000,000 people in Germany have lost everything they possess. The only logical direction in which these people can turn, unless they are directed and controlled, is towards Communism.

The chief characteristic of the German people is that they must have strong leadership, either by one man or by a small body of men. The only man after the Führer who has the complete confidence of the whole German nation, and whom they will follow, is Reichsführer and Chief of the S.S., Heinrich Himmler.

It is realised that there can be no agreement between the Western Allies and a National Socialist government.

For these reasons, the following proposals are made:

(1) The S.S., under Reichsführer Himmler, and other elements, will seize control of Germany and will negotiate an immediate peace with the Western Allies.

(2) They will place under arrest such leading National Socialists as Ribbentrop, Goebbels, Goering, Ley and others, and hand over these persons to the Western Allies.

The position of Hitler raises a special problem, owing to the position he holds in the minds of the German people, and it is suggested that special discussions shall be held to decide upon a solution.

(3) The National Socialist German Workers' Party shall be dissolved and disbanded, and a new party embodying the best points of National Socialism with other ideals shall be set up in its place, to be tentatively called the New German Socialist Party.

In return, we who formulate these proposals, ask that:

(1) The Western Allies shall combine with the German armed forces to overthrow the Russians and destroy the Bolshevist menace.

(2) They will give their support to the new German régime to be formed under Reichsführer Himmler.

Having obtained the Prime Minister's agreement, and possible counter proposals, I was to return to Switzerland immediately and communicate them to Cristopher, who in turn would communicate them to the people concerned. The greatest possible speed was urged to reduce unnecessary slaughter and waste of material on both sides and to check any further advance by Russia.

CHAPTER 20

NIGHT TRAIN TO MUNICH

I

I AM not quite sure whether Martin Bormann made his broadcast authorising the voluntary evacuation of women and children from Berlin on Easter Saturday or Easter Sunday. Whenever it was, the result was the same. On Easter Monday all the great Berlin stations for the west and south were so congested that Pretsch, in consultation with Willy, decided that our departure should be further delayed until the Tuesday after Easter.

Accordingly, on the evening of April 3rd, we arrived at seven o'clock at the Anhalter Bahnhof to take the express to Munich. The train was not due out until eight o'clock, but was already so crowded that people were sitting on the buffers, hanging out of the windows and standing on the running-boards. It was impossible to get anywhere near the train.

At eleven o'clock every evening a military train left the station, supposedly for the south. But no one could say with any certainty where it would eventually arrive. Willy, having discovered that it might pass through Landshut, not a great distance from Munich, decided that we should risk it, rather than wait another day, when we might have the same experience; for although we had been provided with 'highest priority' papers by the S.S., signed by General Schellenberg himself, station and military officials merely waved them aside.

At quarter to ten we joined the queue at the barrier waiting for this military train. When it eventually steamed out, it was crowded with officers and men of all ranks and all Services, including several generals with their staffs and many high-ranking officers of the S.S. Again and again I heard the word *Drunten*, meaning 'under' or 'below', but not until I reached Munich did I recognise its significance; that it was, in fact, the code word for the famous southern redoubt, which was ultimately a failure. As the train drew out of the station in the darkness, the sirens sounded. Rapidly gathering speed, we drew away from Berlin as the bombs began to fall. No flak went up, though searchlights made brilliant criss-cross patterns in the sky. The Mosquitoes had come a little later than usual.

By the time we had boarded the train there were no vacant seats, so we sat on our suitcases in the close-packed corridor. Willy had all his possessions with him in two suitcases; mine were in a suitcase and a rucksack. It was a miserable journey and we stopped at innumerable stations; no one got out, but many tried to get in. At each stop the train's destination was changed, so we decided to wait and see how close we could get to Munich before we got off.

As soon as it was daylight the nervous tension of the passengers heightened. With maddening slowness the train crawled on, the passengers now thinning, now increasing. But night fell again, and the R.A.F. had not attacked us.

At a quarter to three in the morning we got out on to the platform at Dachau. Shivering with cold, hungry and thirsty, we stamped up and down the platform, waiting for the shuttle-service to take us the twenty remaining miles to Munich. For the last three months no main-line trains had been running into Munich station, which had been almost annihilated by the R.A.F. Shuttle-services from improvised sidings ran out to the larger stations and junctions within a radius of twenty miles of the town.

Presently the train came in empty and we entered a second-class Pullman compartment. At four o'clock we arrived at Munich, and joining the stream of weary fighting men, passed out of the battered station and took refuge in a forces' canteen until morning.

II

Before we left Berlin it had been arranged that at Munich I should transmit test messages by radio to the Havel Institute between ten o'clock and midday, in order to get used to working alone with my transmitter under 'field' conditions. For this reason I had brought with me a set identical with the 'chocolate-box' set. In these uncertain days, when triggers were pulled first and questions asked afterwards, it would have been too risky to have tried to do this from our lodgings, and we had been instructed to go to S.S. Headquarters in Munich, so that I might operate from there. At eight o'clock, therefore, leaving our baggage in the cloakroom, we went out into the daylight of Munich.

If Berlin was difficult to describe, Munich is easy. Imagine a sprawling city of over 800,000 inhabitants, of fine sixteenth and seventeenth century houses, magnificent churches, and with more museums than any other city in the world; with palaces that had housed Bavarian kings for centuries; a city of broad streets, great modern shops, and huge factories on the outskirts, with a wide fast-flowing river through the middle of it. Then imagine a gigantic heap of rubble covering hundreds of thousands of acres, from which arose gaunt, derelict fingers of brickwork – a scene of chaotic devastation and almost all of it wrought in a single day and night during two raids on January 7th, 1945.

I had been in Munich before National Socialism, which it suckled, came to power. Willy had spent many months of study there. But on this dull April morning neither of us knew which way to turn. All the familiar landmarks were gone, and we were lost as surely as if we were in the midst of a desert. There was not a house, a shop, a church, a museum, monument, hotel or hospital, in the whole of Munich that had not been damaged or completely destroyed.

Yet the streets were crowded with people – people who lived improvised lives in improvised homes, offices, and shops. Trams were running in some of the less impeded streets, and a steam train, with roughly-built wooden waggons, brought the people from the suburbs to the middle of the city. There was an abundance of food, for apart from the fact that Bavaria is a great agricultural region, the Nazis invariably bought peace among badly bombed civilians by allowing them extra rations. The people were shabby, pale and haggard. Every other woman seemed pregnant, and the children were starved and rickety. Their playgrounds were the mountains of rubble, the crazy walls and the foul static-water tanks.

Eventually we found a tram going out to the residential suburb where the S.S. Headquarters were situated. Here a few houses stood more or less undamaged, and after a search we found the place. On the steps two men where standing talking; the shrill voice of one of them struck a chord in my memory. I looked up and saw that it was Fischer, my old enemy from Dulag West, his shaven head uncovered and his face white and drawn. The Frankfurt Gestapo were evidently coming down into the redoubt. I looked him full in the face, but he gave no sign of recognition. I was tempted to make myself known and to ask if Commissar Bütt and Walter Schmitt were also here; but I resisted, feeling that even now he would stop at nothing to have my head.

We were greeted by a Lieutenant Weiner, who had heard of our coming but had received no particulars. The local commander was away, but was expected back in the afternoon, so Weiner could do nothing more than give me permission to set up my radio. He also obtained rooms for us at the only hotel open in Munich, the Excelsior, and sent us back with one of his N.C.O.s so that we should have no difficulty.

The commander returned the following morning, and when he had interviewed us, sent us to a Captain Schultz, who was expert at putting agents over the Swiss frontier. At Schultz's office we found him burning papers, before leaving for Bregenz on the frontier. When we explained briefly what we wanted, he told us to call and see him there, and he would have everything arranged. He warned us, however, that we should have to be very careful, and that British agents 'lurked behind every corner' at Bregenz.

Every morning between ten and noon I set up my radio, but failed to make a single contact. There was great confusion in Berlin by this time. The Russians were concentrating on Danzig with a fury that was taken to indicate that the final attack on Berlin would begin at any moment. The Americans were appearing in the most unexpected places, and Berlin was in danger of being cut off from the south. On Saturday, April 7th, we heard that Paeffgan and his department had arrived *Drunten*; but there was still no sign of Cristopher in Munich.

CHAPTER 21

OVER THE BORDER

Willy had received orders that with or without Cristopher, we were to leave for Switzerland on April 10th. So at a quarter to four on the afternoon of that day, we left Munich by the shuttle service to pick up the main-line train at Päsing, a suburban town twenty miles out. The railways by this time were even more disorganised than they had been the week before, when we had left Berlin.

We had been told that the shuttle train would take us to Kempten, where we should change for the Bregenz express. It was rumoured that the Americans were now in Augsburg, and were fanning out north-east towards Regensburg, and south-east towards Munich. They were travelling at speed along the *Autobahn*, and might even cut the railway we were on.

At Landsberg, however, it was 'all change' – our train was not going to Kempten. Five minutes after we got down, the alert sounded, so instead of waiting an hour for the direct train to Kempten, we took the local one to Buchlö. Just after midnight we managed to squeeze into the corridor of an express, and as dawn broke the train drew into Bregenz station. Cold and miserable, we went to the buffet, only to find that it would not open for half an hour. So, amid dust and upturned chairs, we sat down to wait, and in a few minutes every place was taken.

In order to be as thorough as possible, I had decided to eat nothing until passing the Swiss frontier, so that I should be really hungry when I told the police my story. I was also extremely tired, and kept falling asleep over the table, to be awakened each time by a dig from Willy. But after two or three cups of ersatz coffee I felt better.

According to the instructions that had been given to Willy, we were to wait in Bregenz until midday, then take the train to a village called Götzis, where we were to enquire for Herr Hans Eggers, who would give us further instructions.

This we did, and at one o'clock found Hans Eggers in his house behind the local school. The fragile man who met us hardly seemed like the typical master-spy of fiction. He was white-haired, soft-spoken and timid, and wore gold-rimmed half-lenses on the tip of his nose. The interior of the cottage, though not luxurious, placed him at once in the comfortable class. The name-plate on his door proclaimed 'Hans Eggers — Weaver' but there was no loom in his workshop, only a covered sewing-machine, a trestle-table and an ironing-board.

His instructions were that we were to take the train to

a place called Feldkirch, where we would be met by the captain of the local German frontier guard, who would tell us what to do.

After lunching at the inn, we hung about the village until the evening, when we went back to Eggers' house, he having earlier invited us to return at nine o'clock. There we sat and discussed literature, and in the course of our conversation Eggers told us that James Joyce had once visited his house, and had sat in the chair in which I was sitting at that moment.

At half-past eleven we left and walked through the sleeping, moonlit village to the station, where we boarded the train for Feldkirch.

With the air of conspirators we met the captain of the frontier guard and his lieutenant in the darkened entrance of Feldkirch station. An S.S. man in uniform with a tall, fair-haired, bespectacled civilian, alighting at a small station in the middle of the night could not be mistaken. No one spoke a word as we got into the captain's car and drove to his headquarters. Here we made a careful study of the map.

The place where I was to cross the frontier was about eight miles away, near a village called Bludenz. The captain explained the routine to be followed. He and his lieutenant would drive to a certain spot where there would be a soldier on guard; both officers would leave the car, but I was to remain hidden in the back seat. The lieutenant would go into a house, and the captain would start off on his rounds with the guard. When the captain and the guard had gone, the lieutenant would fetch me from the car and lead me along a path to an empty farmhouse; here I was to wait for the captain. The lieutenant would have gone ahead to see if any Swiss guards were patrolling on the other side of the wire. If all was clear, the captain would take me to a gate in the barrier, which the lieutenant would already have opened.

On the other side of the wire I was to move to the right, and after going about four hundred yards, I should come to a wide stream. I was not to cross this, but to follow it round until I came to a tributary flowing east-to-west into it. This I was to follow until I came to a foot-bridge, which I was to cross, then, keeping beside the first stream, make towards a light which I should see in the distance; this would be the village of Regel. On no account must I cross the stream on my right, or I should find myself back in Germany.

When questioned by the Swiss police, I was to say that I had watched the German guard for some hours during the afternoon at a spot near Feldkirch — this was to avoid compromising the section of the frontier where I should actually cross — then, seizing a favourable opportunity, I had pulled up the lower strands of wire and crawled under the barrier.

When I had been in Paris, Captain Fritz had given me an old suit. On entering the Stalag at Limburg, I had handed all my belongings to Cristopher, who had taken them to his flat in Berlin. I found them when I arrived there, except for my storm-jacket and overcoat, which his wife had generously contributed to the Winter Relief Fund. It was as well, therefore, that while I was in the S.S. Hospital in Paris, I had extracted the wireless code which I had stolen from Hugo.

My clothing now consisted of the old suit given me by Fritz, my army shirt, underclothes and boots – which would support my story that I was an escaped prisoner of war – and a very old overcoat which the Brunswick Gestapo had provided to cover my uniform when I was taken down to the hotel that Sunday afternoon. It was into these clothes that I changed, giving my others to Willy. I had not shaved or washed since before leaving Munich, so as well as feeling extremely hungry, I looked dirty and haggard.

During January and February I had written a further account of my operations to bring them up to date. I had camouflaged it from the others in the camp by beginning it as a novel, so after the first day or two my writing would not give rise to comment. Having finished it, I had taken it to the lavatory – the only place where I had any privacy – and sewn it into the lining of my military greatcoat, so wherever I went it would be with me. On my leaving Oflag 79 it had accompanied me, undiscovered, to Berlin, where I had kept it up to date every day until the journey to Munich. Now it was hanging in a special bag which I had made for it and fixed into the middle of the back of my old overcoat. My experience of being searched had taught me that searchers never ran their hands down the middle of the back. Unless the Swiss police searched me very thoroughly, which I thought would be unlikely, I did not think they would find it. It was a foolish risk to take, nevertheless; but I was extremely keen to get it through, because attached to it were spare photostat copies of my radio-plan, as well as my procedure and call-sign, which I had managed to purloin. The bag also contained my Berlin identity card – no one had thought of asking me to return it – and a copy of the S.M.O.'s report to the German doctors, which Cristopher had procured for me when I had said I would like to have the terms of it made clear.

When I was dressed, I said goodbye to Willy, and almost sick with excitement and nerves, I got into the car with the two German officers. Everything passed off as arranged, and at approximately twenty minutes past three on the night of April 12th/13th, they gave me their good wishes, and I passed through the gate in the barrier.

It was a tremendous moment. For 898 days, from

November 5th, 1942, to April 12th, 1945, I had been under sentence of death. At any moment of that period I might have been put against a wall and shot, or else strung from a rope, or been beheaded.

Now I was free! But though the threat was gone, I could not really believe my good fortune. It seemed quite incredible that I had cheated the Germans of my life, hoodwinked them for nearly three years with fantastic stories, pitted my brain against the best of their Intelligence, and having gained their confidence, was now carrying a message from the infamous Himmler to Winston Churchill. I felt sure, even as I lurched back from the edge of the stream which I had almost walked into, that soon I should wake and find myself in a prison cell; but if it was a dream, it was not yet finished.

In the distance below I saw twinkling lights and went gradually towards them. Though the night was dark, there were thousands of stars overhead, and the air was soft and warm. I followed the stream, which was lined with bushes, for about five kilometres, till I came at last to the Lichtenstein hamlet of Regel. I had not seen a soul.

Lights burned in the streets and in every window, both upstairs and down. I wandered round for some time trying to find a policeman or a frontier guard to whom I might surrender, and presently came to a large, covered, wooden bridge. As I stepped on to it, I heard a man cough. Half-way across the bridge, I could see a closed gate, and as I went nearer to it I saw a soldier in a German steel helmet.

I ran back quietly on to Lichtenstein territory, for my geography of the neighbourhood was extremely uncertain, and I thought the river here might be the boundary between Germany and Switzerland, as it is nearer Bregenz.

Then I heard an engine throbbing somewhere and went in search of it. I found the noise came from a flour mill, but no one seemed to be about. So I lay down beside the wall of a barn to try to sleep; but the ground was wet and the air was becoming colder, so I got up again and continued to walk about.

It was not until half-past five that I found a Swiss frontier-guard – the Swiss Army protects the German-Lichtenstein boundary – in the middle of the village, and said to him in German:

'I am an English prisoner of war, an officer. I have escaped from Germany.'

'So?' he said, and walked away to a nearby house. I was not going to let him get away, so I followed him, and together we threw handfuls of earth up at the windows. Presently one of them was opened and a head was thrust through.

'An English officer, prisoner of war from Germany,' said the guard.

'Take him to the post. I'll come at once,' said the head at the window.

'Come,' said the guard; then, as though it were an afterthought, 'Are you armed?'

'No,' I said, but he ran his hands over me to satisfy himself.

We came to the post, and in the light of the guardroom he looked at me searchingly.

'Cigarette?'

I took one, and he lit it for me. Then he asked for my particulars, including my grandmother's maiden name. To avoid embarrassing the Swiss authorities, and for reasons of British security, I had decided for the time being to remain Captain John de Witt. I realised also that the International Red Cross archives at Geneva would have my particulars as a prisoner of war under that name.

The guard's colleague soon arrived, bringing with him a covered basket, from which he took a flask of hot coffee, half a loaf, butter, cheese and jam.

'You'll be hungry,' he said. 'Eat and drink.'

He then went to the telephone, and after a brief wait, we crossed the wooden bridge. As he went over it I looked at the Swiss guard and saw that his helmet was shaped like a German soldier's.

On the far side of the river we were in Switzerland. Here I waited in a guard hut, where soldiers pressed cigarettes and coffee upon me.

Presently a panting policeman arrived on a bicycle. 'Please come quickly,' he said, speaking urgently in French, 'or we shall miss the train.'

As we went along, the policeman on his bicycle with me trotting beside him, we heard the train approaching. I could go no faster, so he jumped off and thrust his bicycle at me. 'Here, take it. Ride!' he said, and ran along beside me to the station.

We alighted from the train at Buchs twenty minutes later, and I was taken to the local gaol, where the gaoler emptied my pockets, but did not search me.

'What are these?' he asked, picking up the secret ink tablets.

'Aspirin,' I said.

'I'm afraid I must lock you up,' said the gaoler, 'until the captain comes. We've had a lot of Germans trying to get through as British prisoners during the last few days. It won't be for long though, if your identity can be checked.'

So I was taken to a spacious cell and locked in. The gaoler had returned my razor and washing kit, so I washed and shaved, then got into bed exhausted and soon fell asleep.

I had been asleep about an hour when the rattle of a key in the lock awoke me and the gaoler brought a police officer into the cell. As he spoke to me in German, I replied in German. Then in the middle of what he was saying, he switched to French: again I followed him. Then without warning, he broke into English, and after a few moments he smiled and said; 'Yes, you're English all right.'

He apologised for having to keep me in a cell, but there was no other accommodation. It would only be until the next day, when I should be going to Geneva with four Frenchmen, who had arrived earlier in the week. I was free, however, to come and go as I pleased, as long as I did not go near the railway station, where there were some German police, most of them really Gestapo officials. I said that I should be very grateful if the captain would get in touch with the British Minister in Berne. This, he said, had already been done.

I was not particularly anxious to go out, so I stayed on my bed until I was fetched an hour later and taken to the police office at the station. Here I was asked for particulars of myself. Meanwhile, the captain had bought me a packet of English cigarettes and some matches and magazines. When my questionnaire was completed, I was medically examined, then, still being very weary, I returned to my cell, had lunch and again fell asleep on the bed.

At six o'clock the gaoler brought my supper. 'You will be leaving with the Frenchmen for Berne tomorrow,' he said. 'I shall call you at half-past five. Your train leaves at ten minutes to seven.'

Early next morning I left with the four Frenchmen for Berne, by way of Zurich, where we changed.

As I was waiting there on the platform, a well-dressed woman came up to me and handed me a packet of cigarettes. 'Give my love to England,' she said with a smile. I thought at first that she might be one of Cristopher's agents and that I should find a message in the cigarettes; but there was nothing.

Wherever I went it was the same. Time and again I was the object of genuine and spontaneous kindness by the Swiss, which touched me deeply.

It was just after midday when the Frenchmen and I parted company in Berne.

CHAPTER 22

BACK TO BASE

I HAVE always liked to imagine that 13 is my lucky number. It was now Friday, April 13th. Perhaps this combination was too much for providence. At any rate, there now began a series of delays which, with the end of my troubles at last in sight, drove me to the verge of desperation.

Immediately on arriving at the Legation in Berne, I told Brigadier Cartwright, the Military Attaché, of my special mission and who I really was. I said that I did not wish to say more than was necessary to him or to the Minister, and made it plain that I must give my message personally to Mr Churchill. I emphasised also that time was the vital factor.

Brigadier Cartwright took me off to lunch at his flat, where he made it clear that I would be well advised to acquaint the Minister with the full details of my message. After lunch he offered me a hot bath, and suggested that I should think things over.

At three o'clock I saw the Minister, Mr (now Sir) Clifford Norton, K.C.M.G. Having given him a rough outline of the situation, without really doing justice either to myself or to Himmler's proposals, I suggested that I should write it all out. The Minister agreed, so I wrote a detailed account of what had taken place, stressing once again that only I could deal with the matter and that time was all-important. At six-thirty that evening I handed the Minister my report.

'I will condense it,' he said, 'have it encoded, and send it off.'

'And what about me?' I asked.

'The earliest we can get an answer back about you is Tuesday – four days. It may even take a week,' he said.

I did my best to emphasise the urgency of my mission, but I had a feeling that it seemed less important to the Minister than I believed it to be.

'They are idiots,' he said, 'if they think Churchill will ever consider such terms.'

I knew that, of course. Yet if I could have reached the Prime Minister, I am sure he would have made some use of the situation. Though neither the Minister nor Brigadier Cartwright seemed much impressed, an effort was made to get the radio parcel; but if the chocolate box ever arrived from Cristopher, I was never told.

Throughout Saturday, Sunday, and Monday, I was interrogated by the Air and Military Attachés. On Tuesday I was given twenty pounds, and shopped all the morning, buying presents for my family, which I had delivered to the Legation.

When I got back to England, I found my pay had already been debited with twenty pounds. So it seemed that when something of really vital importance was concerned, the transmission of messages was not so slow after all.

I left Berne by the night express for Geneva on April 17th. It was a welcome change from the filthy, crowded trains to which I had become accustomed. I had a first class compartment to myself, and dressed once again in British uniform, I rolled myself up in my greatcoat and slept.

It was about half-past six when I arrived in Geneva, and after rolls and coffee in the station buffet, I picked up four Indians, tubercular convalescents whom the Legation had been trying to get back to England for months. At the Swiss frontier station Swiss officers saw me through the customs.

At half-past eight I had completed the French customs formalities, but the Indians had left all their papers behind with the Swiss. I had my movement order, but I did not know if the French would let the Indians proceed without personal papers. As the station master had not yet arrived, and as we had an hour to wait for the Lyons train, I went in search of the British Consul, so that he could telegraph for the Indians' papers to be sent to Lyons immediately; but there was no British Consul in the town.

Outside the station I caught sight of two American

322

sergeants in a truck, and learned from them that there was an American Consul.

'Jump in,' they said, 'and we'll drive you to his office.'

But it was too early; the Consul's office was still closed; so they drove me back to the station.

Before we parted I told them my predicament, and they both put into words my own feelings, which by this time were quite unprintable. However, the station master was now on duty, and I explained the situation to him. Very kindly he endorsed my movement order with the necessary particulars and said that if I had any trouble, the French authorities were to telephone him.

Owing to damaged bridges, we had to go miles out of our way, via Chambèry and Grenoble, so that it was seven o'clock in the evening before we arrived at Lyons, by which time we were more dead than alive. At Lyons, as the British Liaison officer did not know we were coming, he had made no arrangements for the remainder of our journey; so another day was lost.

The following morning at the airfield they quoted an order which had just arrived, forbidding the flying of p.o.w.s to England without briefing from London. So we left for Paris on the evening train.

It was nine o'clock on the morning of April 20th when we arrived there. Here I was seen by a Canadian Intelligence Corps Officer, the first really energetic person I had yet met since I had left Swiss hands. He hurried out to SHAEF Headquarters and came back in the afternoon to say that he had arranged a place for me on a 'plane leaving the next day – nine days after I had crossed the German-Swiss frontier. Early the following afternoon I stepped out on to British soil, 910 days after leaving it. Of those days I had spent 901 in Germany or German-occupied territory.

As I drove through the streets of suburban London, and saw the London Transport buses, the bakers' carts and the little houses, all the horrors of my captivity were swept away. I could not then put into words the feelings that I experienced on that journey through London, nor can I do so now. The language of lovers finds expression in the eyes, and I looked at London with the eyes of a lover. I was home again.

The following morning I began my report to Military Intelligence – and finished answering their questions, at the rate of six or seven hours a day, a fortnight later. No mention was made of my seeing the Prime Minister, and I do not even know whether he ever heard of me or of my mission; by this time I did not greatly care.

With the exception of the Wing-Commander, who was now a Group-Captain, and the Pay Officer, not one of my old friends remained with S.O.E. Major Larch had returned to his regiment and was now a Lieutenant-Colonel serving on the Continent. My area chief had returned to civilian life, and I was a stranger among strangers who had little interest in me.

The Air Ministry, on the other hand, treated me with considerable courtesy. Air-Commodore Grant, Director of Intelligence (Operations), and the late Wing-Commander Rose, the German expert, received me at the Air Ministry and expressed their appreciation of what I had done.

Sometimes while I was training I used to think that if, when it was all over, my children asked me what I did in the war, I should be able to answer with modest pride, 'I did this or that.' In my Frankfurt cell I used to imagine that I heard them asking that question, and myself replying, 'I made 67,000 paper bags for Germany.'

In my more cynical moments I feel that this is a fair comment on my war service. For, discounting all that I had to go through, what did my efforts amount to? The only information which appeared to be of any use was that which allowed Intelligence to identify and seize a circle of German agents, who were to have remained in Paris after the liberation; and the particulars I had supplied of German codes and secret inks.

But I had a brief moment of triumph, when the report of Count Bernadotte's negotiations with Himmler was announced.

In the meantime Allied soldiers had continued to lay down their lives.

RONALD SETH (1911–1985)

When Ronald Seth returned to England after making his escape, he was not unmarked by the extreme deprivation and hardship that he had experienced (his belt – which his daughter still possesses – was only eighteen inches long). He would suffer from ill health for the remainder of his days, but this did not prevent him from leading a full and productive life.

After the war, he worked for a short time in the Ministry of Works and then spent a couple of years teaching at a school in Guernsey. Immediately before the outbreak of the war he had written *Baltic Corner*, an account of his travels in Estonia and of Estonian culture, and he would devote himself fully to a writing career after 1950. He was a fluent and prolific writer, and wrote a great variety of books, both for adults and children, specialising for the most part in the history of espionage and the history of the Second World War (though he became something of an expert, too, on the history of witchcraft trials and popular lore about witches). He led a peripatetic existence, being obliged to travel to the US in order to conduct research for many of his books (and would often make use of the time on the boat there and back to write short works for children).

His wife, Josephine, died in 1964, and he would later marry again. He died in 1985, and was survived by his second wife, Barbara, and his children Christopher and Joanna.

Ronald Seth and his family in 1945, six months after his return from Germany

'LEVAVI OCULOS', A POEM BY RONALD SETH

Referring, in *A Spy Has No Friends*, to the period in which he awaited his execution in Tallinn Central Prison, Seth remarked that 'I found that I had no doubts at all about God's understanding of man's sins and weaknesses, and with this realisation my feelings of fear disappeared . . . Most of my thoughts during these hours were not centred on God but on my family.' It is possible to gain a fuller insight into what Seth felt and thought at this time from a remarkable document, recording a poem that Seth composed in his cell as he waited for death. Seth remarked of the poem: 'I began these lines in 22 December, 1942 in the Central Prison of Tallinn, Estonia. I had just been told that I was to be hanged publicly on 24 December. I began it to divert my thoughts from the end. I had no writing materials, so I committed it to memory. After the respite granted me by the failure of the gallows to function, during the next two years I added to the poem and when at last I came to write it down in August, 1945, after my return to England, I found that there were only a few flaws of scansion and rhythm which I wished to alter.'

'*Levavi Oculos*' reveals more of the anxiety and anguish of this experience than the rather laconic account in *A Spy Has No Friends*, but it bears out his claim that his thoughts moved from an initial anxiety about his 'sins and weaknesses', his condition before God, to an overwhelming concern with his family, and his love for his wife, his 'Best Beloved'. It is by invoking the imagined presence of those he loves that he is able to dispel his fear.

An abridged version of the poem is published here, with all excisions marked by asterisks. The title, '*Levavi Oculos*', is a reference to Psalm 121, *Levavi oculos meos in montes* – 'I lift up my eyes to the hills; from whence is my help to come? My help comes from the Lord, the maker of heaven and earth.'

LEVAVI OCULOS

It is not fear of pain, the hangman's jerk,
The bullet's searing burn
That turns
This living flesh into gross stinking corpse.
This living flesh turned to a stinking corpse?
Nay. Even now there is a putrefactory stench
Upon my corpse that is but skeleton and skin,
Entrails and a very little blood,
And many nerves, and, above all,
Consciousness.
It is not fear of pain, nor yet of death,
But of these last few hours of life.
For in these three months past I have feared life.

Why then must I have courage?
                              Why, because
    I have loved life!
And even as I welcome now sweet death
    I must dam up my thoughts
Which hanker after love and warmth,

331

Friendship and comfortable joys,
Laughter and purifying tears,
The touch of love,
Soft voices,
And the shrill joy of my children who
Dance in the sun, laugh in the rain.

Left sixteen hours of life,
And an eternity of death.
I must dam up my thoughts!
But how?
Pray, sinful wretch!
Prepare to meet thy Lord!
Our Father which art in heaven.
And when ye pray, pray not as the Pharisees
And Scribes, O hypocrites!
'Thank God I'm not as other men.'[1]
Ought I to fear God then, since even now
I have begun my journey's final stage
To meet Him? Do I not fear my sins
Will shut me out of Heaven?

*

[1] The references here are to Matthew 6, and Luke 18:11, in which Jesus instructs his followers how to pray, urging humility before God.

If suffering can shrive a man of sin
My sufferings have blanched my soul lamb-white.
   Agnus Dei qui tollis peccata mundi.[2]

*

The slip-slop of the guard's worn boots
   Comes shuffling down the corridor of Time,
And slithers to a stop outside my door.
   The hatch falls with a jolting clash,
A hand thrusts through a dried-up slice of bread
   (Two ounces of rye bread, black bread) retreats
And reappears now with a steaming mug of boiling
   water.
I go and take my midday meal, and hiss,
Crouched down to look at the old man
Hiss in the native tongue:
'What's it to be, Old One, the firing squad?'
He glances each way down the corridor,
Then thrusts his face in mine, and through a cloud
Of rough and reeky vodka, hisses back:
'No, son, it's hanging, and in public too.'

---

[2] A reference to the litany introduced into the Latin Mass in the seventh century, beginning '*Agnus Dei qui tollis peccata mundi, miserere nobis*', 'Lamb of God, who takes away the sins of the world, have mercy on us.'

The last words make me slop the precious drink;
The water scalds my hand, I feel it burn
But only with the far lobes of my brain.

*

Tomorrow's joke — me dancing at a short rope's
    end!
Honour for me, honour of martyrdom.

What blithering rot!
I'd still prefer to live.

*

Hail Holy Mary, full of Grace, I prayed,
Blessed be thy womb's fruit! Pray God for me
That this poor slice of bread fend off the pain
Of empty belly, poor male fruitless belly,
Until the next slice comes.

Some days the Holy Mother heard my plea.
And God performed the miracle again.
But there were other days when heaving ache
Incessantly gnawed at the sustenance
    Of my poor soul.
Bewilderment bit sharply at my reason then.

'Oh, does God sleep?' my awful anguish shrieked.
'Wake, wake, thou Omnipresent, wake!
'Can you not hear? Or is it You won't hear?'

Doubt is a fire that burns deep in the soul,
A wildfire crackling, racing to a roar
Before the spray of reason falls to douche it out,
And having finally consumed itself it leaves
Black-charred remains from which a phoenix-faith
But rears itself with timid forwardness through fear
To quivering new-life through fearsome labour-
    pangs
So that the newest miracle can scarce provide
    Encouragement to ever deeper faith.

What fires of Hell have I to fear (Good Man)
    Who have been scorched by many fires of
Heaven?

*

Let me forget the end in my remembering
The past beginning and the middle past.

The day's light fades – I cannot see the stars
    But they are there, I know, and night comes down

As these last dogged hours relentlessly
    Pulse on with every second heart-beat of the past.
There was once, that I did not hate the night
    But weary hours of painful wakingness
Have brought me longing for the day's
    Realities, cold though they are
Yet warmer than the unlit fantasies
    Of the dawn hours,
The hours when all the world sleeps but oneself.

*

One early morning at the year's first spring
In Henry's Cambridge chapel,[3] I knelt down
To hear the Mass. The pale sun's slanting beams
Caught, held and magnified the splendid wealth
Of gold and scarlet, purple, green and blue
(The Virgin's blue) that round the altar moves
Doing obeisance to the Sacred Host,[4]
For moments, my devotion in suspense,
My very soul was held in splendour's thrall,
And, for the first time, was the exhortation clear
'Give Glory unto God.'

[3] The chapel of King's College, Cambridge, built by Henry VI.
[4] The 'host' is the bread consecrated in the Eucharistic rite.

The moonlight on the Lake at Friar's Crag,[5]
The Best Beloved's soft, translucent voice
Reciting one's own adolescent lines:

Do you remember how the moon
An hour before her midnight noon
Made shadow monsters flit around
Over the lake, above the ground?

And there was pride
In the achievement of those lines:
But greater pride
In the possession of the Best Beloved.

There is the tramp of boots upon stone flags
There is the raucous clash of key in lock.
A name is called; a voice returns reply;
A heavy door clangs shut, and bolts shriek home,
The key clicks in the lock.
So down the corridor they come.

Into my own lock clashes key,
The heavy door swings wide,

[5] Ronald Seth courted his first wife, Josephine, at Friar's Crag, in the
Lake District, and he would scatter her ashes there after her death.

And there I see the Ancient Guard
(Who calls my death a joke)
By whose side stands his chief.
The old man nods to me,
And mumbles through his thinned-out teeth:
'He won't be here tomorrow.'
The chief looks at his list, and ticks my name,
And after momentary hesitation comes,
His hand outstretched, into my cell,
And as he clasps my hand he says to me:
'My people will remember in their hearts
Your sacrifice – for all time!
May God go with you, friend.'
He steps back and salutes, and fierce, hot tears
Gather within my eyes, and overflow.
In these last weeks I have not known
Much kindness. Now the friendly hand,
The quiet voice,
Breaks down the hardness I have hedged about my soul.
The door clangs to
The lock clicks home,
A triple pace of boots
Moves past me to the next.

*

'It is not true. They can't do this to me.
'I meant no harm. I will do anything
'If only they will spare my life.
'I am too young to die.
'I'll plead with Them. I'll sell my soul
'If only They will let me live.'

But soon the spasm ends, the weakness goes,
    And a new strength, much stronger than the last,
Pervades my shrinking heart.
    I roll up with infinite care
In the one stinking blanket and lie down
    Upon the sacking stretched on iron frame –
My bed for close on ninety wretched nights –
    For the last time.

God, dare I hope for sleep to pass the time
In unforgetful, sweet oblivion?

I wake at length, my body stiff with cold
As it will be tomorrow night with death.
Above me on the ceiling flares the blinkless gleam
    Of artificial light.

*

How much longer is there to the dawn?
How much of artificiality
Until I reach the real Estate?

*

The door clangs open at the passage end,
    The jack-boots' slow staccato now descends
In loud crescendo scale towards my door.
    This is the moment that all life awaits,
Not mine alone, but Everyman's.

O Courage, sweetest Courage, leave me not!
Come Calm into my soul, and let me go
Into the vast void of eternity
At peace.
Let not my lips in this first kiss of Death
Falter from that warm firmness that they used
When they last kissed in life.
Come, take me! I am ready!
Glad to go!
And in my Death I have like happiness
That I have had in life.
Only let Love follow me to the tomb
To comfort me deep in the dark earth's womb
For the regrets that have seared black my soul.

My arrogance and my philosophy of love,
My talk of sin, my vaunted fearlessness
Of God and the unknown eternity,
My flagrant lust
Are sham,
Veneer of sham,
That there exists in my experience
Strange blacknesses of branded deep regret
For wrongs done to the Best Beloved
That I have not atoned.
If I had life before me, not harsh death,
I would devote my every living hour
Attempting to obliterate the past
Unhappiness I have caused to hurt
The dear heart of the Best Beloved.

No, I do not require to plead with God
For Absolution, but to her who gave
All that she had of love and strength,
Laughter and sympathetic tears
To bolster my own shameful weakness up,
For every hurt I could I did to her.
When I had opportunity to make amends
I let the chance slip by; and now there is no chance
To make erasion of the smallest wrong

My soul itself is tortured with remorse,
That fearful punishment which Time itself
Can never heal.

Oh, your sweet name I carry on my heart
Engraved in myriads of tiny stabs
That cannot be removed even in death.
Have then no fear, Dear Heart; my latest thought
In this quite worthless life will be of you;
And I shall meet the void eternity
Crying your name with anguish.

Yet one last boon I ask,
Knowing that even now
You'll not refuse me.

Give me your hand,
Come with me to the Gate
That opens out of Life
Into grim Death.
Then I shall go
With some semblance at least
Of courage.
For as your hand
Soothed all my fears in life
So now in Death

Will push away my fears.
Then I shall die
As I was wont to live
Drawing from you
My strength.

The calm comes,
And courage lifts my soul
To strength.

Come, take me, I am ready.
Let me go!

Now you can buy any of these other World War II stories from your bookshop or direct from the publisher

Down in the Drink   *Ralph Barker*   £7.99
Among those who fought in the ferocious battles for the skies during the Second World War, some – shot down, or forced to ditch – had to confront an exceptionally pitiless enemy: the sea. The accounts of heroism and endurance in *Down in the Drink* match any from World War II. They are stories of men from all corners of the British Commonwealth fighting for survival against unimaginable odds. Their experiences give stirring proof that there is no limit to human courage.

Boldness Be My Friend   *Richard Pape*   £7.99
Aggressive, impetuous and dauntless, Richard Pape was never going to sit out the war in a Nazi prison. Captured and imprisoned when his bomber crashed, his daring escape was only the beginning of a long struggle for freedom. *Boldness Be My Friend* is a gripping tale of astonishing courage.

The Honour and the Shame   *John Kenneally*   £7.99
John Kenneally won the VC in 1943 for a solo attack on a whole company of Panzer Grenadiers. Years later, he confessed that he had joined the Irish Guards under an assumed name after deserting his original regiment. *The Honour and the Shame* brings to life the adventures of a freewheeling youth and the horror and exhilaration of the battlefield.

Odette   *Jerrard Tickell*   £7.99
In the darkest days of the Second World War, a young Frenchwoman, a wife and mother, became a secret agent. Leaving England to aid the French Resistance, she was betrayed, tortured, consigned to a concentration camp and sentenced to death. Yet she kept, in the abyss, her hope. *Odette* tells the story of an ordinary woman who, when tested, displayed an extraordinary courage and compassion.

TRUE STORIES FROM WORLD WAR II
Real heroes. Real courage.

To order, simply call 01235 400 414
visit our website: www.madaboutbooks.com
or email orders@bookpoint.co.uk

Prices and availability are subject to change without notice.